A Kid's Guide to Movies

by J. M. Clements

Scholastic Inc.

New York   Toronto   London   Auckland   Sydney
Mexico City   New Delhi   Hong Kong   Buenos Aires

Dedication

To Elena and Marius

About the Author

J.M. Clements is an author, scriptwriter and translator. He once played the bad guy in a cartoon, which explains a lot.

Thanks to

Jeremy Clarke, Michael Clements, Penny Clements, Chelsey Fox, Marcus Hearn, Charlotte Howard, Matthew Johnson, Steve Livermore, Adam Newell, Kate Pankhurst, Jim Swallow

ISBN 0-439-43117-4

Copyright © 2002 Jonathan Clements

12 11 10 9 8 7 6 5 4 3 2 1   2 3 4 5 6 7/0

Book design by Alison Withey

Typeset by Dorchester Typesetting Group Ltd.

Printed in the U.S.A.

First Scholastic printing, November 2002

Introduction

Adults don't know it all. Some of them even think that what they enjoyed as kids will be perfect for you. But it might not be. You might not really feel like watching an old Disney film where everyone has silly haircuts, or something in black-and-white — just because it's supposed to be "better than the remake." This book is for YOU, which is why it contains:

FAST-FORWARD ⏩ *suggestions so you can edit out the boring parts.*

Plus:

- Things you can say to impress or annoy adults in the room.
- In-jokes and mistakes to watch out for.
- Ideas for themed video marathons for sleepovers and rainy days.
- Critiques of the DVD extras. DVDs cost more to buy or rent, and you want your money's worth.
- Escape from the KIDS section: some checklists of the best films in genres supposedly for grown-ups, but actually perfect for you.
- Fascinating film facts, gossip, and some of those weird film job titles explained.

And the Doctor is IN to deal with bad cases of "sequelitis." Some studios think you'll buy any old trash just because it's "Your Favorite Film, Part Two." Fight the power!

The book also has the following icons as a guide:

 Guaranteed not to embarrass you in front of your parents, or vice versa. Will keep everyone entertained.

Nightmare-causing content liable to give younger family members the heebie-jeebies. No matter what the rating says, rent with care (and only if you really want a scary night!).

 If the show stops for a decent song, so can you.

A few notes before we start:
VHS

You're a child of the digital age, but these antique videocassettes are still around in large numbers and will often be the medium of choice for adults. Humor the grown-ups — they probably own a lot of them, and they don't want to admit that they have Stone Age film technology.

DVDs

DVDs cost more to buy and more to rent. So why should you have to settle for the same experience you get on VHS? A DVD should have plenty of decent extras, otherwise you should just save money and get the tape.

Ratings and data

Each film is rated with between one and five stars:

✪✪✪✪✪ Perfect. Buy it.

✪✪✪✪ Great. Rent it.

✪✪✪ Average. Borrow it.

✪✪ Could do better. Beats school, but only just.

✪ Awful. They should pay you to watch.

These ratings are just my personal opinion. You will probably disagree. That's what people do. They always say "He must be joking!?" "Oh, no, he's an idiot!" etc., etc. This is probably why publishers insist on them, so everyone has something to talk about. To be honest, the same applies to all the information in this book — the movie world moves very fast. Releases are brought out, taken off the shelves, or altered at short notice — treat this book as a guide, but not as gospel. Check for yourself before you buy anything, in case things have changed since this book was written. Tell us what you think about your favorite film — perhaps we have even left it out! **(movies@doublecluck.com)**

We've also included the censor's ratings. Most of the films in this book are rated "G" — that is, for general audiences, so we've only included ratings where they don't conform to the norm:

PG   Parental guidance suggested.

PG-13 Parents strongly cautioned. Some material may be inappropriate for children under 13.

R   Restricted. Under 17 requires accompanying parent or adult guardian.

Christmas means carnage (as Babe would say)

It would be perfectly easy to fill this entire book with Christmas spin-offs and Christmas movies, but I've left most of them out. This is a book about repeat viewing, and Christmas should only come once a year. Most Christmas "specials" are simply retreads of the same story anyway — see **A CHRISTMAS CAROL**.

So now on to the really important part — the films themselves . . . arranged in alphabetical order, of course!

The Addams Family
PG-13
Paramount Pictures Corp.   1991
DVD; VHS

Devilishly handsome Gomez, his icy, drop-*dead* gorgeous wife, Morticia, nasty children Wednesday and Pugsley, Lurch the butler, and handy pet Thing are the Addamses, a creepy American family. But their lawyer, Alford, is the truly nasty one. He plans to cheat them out of their fortune with the aid of Gordon Craven, a man who looks just like Gomez's long-lost brother Fester. Not much scope for fast-forwarding, since the whole film is a succession of quick gags. If you don't like what you see, just wait a minute. Watch for the passenger who glares out at Gomez when he's trying to crash his trains — it's the director Barry Sonnenfeld. Nothing but two trailers as "extras" on the DVD — that's horrific.

 Star rating: ✪✪

Addams Family Values
PG-13
Paramount Pictures Corp.   1993
VHS

There's a new arrival at the Addams Family home ("Is it a girl? Is it a boy? It's an Addams!"), and the jealous Wednesday and Pugsley are sent away to summer camp while the parents adjust to Pubert, their new baby. But the family is under threat once again, this time from a nanny who is determined to con Uncle Fester out of his fortune. Just a *little* bit better than the first movie, which is surprising, since the plot's hardly all that different. Look out for the "Harmony Hut" where bad little campers are sent.

Can you imagine anything worse than putting the Addams children in a room with the Brady Bunch?

 Star rating: ✪✪✪

The Adventures of Elmo in Grouchland

Columbia Pictures   1999
DVD; VHS

Elmo fights with his friend Zoe on Sesame Street, losing his precious blue blanket in Oscar the Grouch's trash can. He and his friends go to Grouchland to look and discover that the blanket has been stolen by Huxley the Toy Thief, who lives on Mount Pickanose. Good fun for the young ones, but if you're old enough to be reading this book, you're probably too old for this film. The DVD includes an introduction from Elmo and Bug, as well as a "Making of" documentary.

Star rating: ✪✪

The Adventures of the Great Mouse Detective

Buena Vista Pictures Distribution, Inc.   1986
VHS

In Victorian London, the dastardly professor Ratigan kidnaps toy maker Flaversham, forcing him to make a mouse-robot to overthrow the queen. Basil the detective and his assistant Dawson (who both live beneath a famous Baker Street address) are hired by Olivia Flaversham to rescue her father, and the chase begins. A soundtrack of wonderful songs completes the package. Spooky-voiced

Vincent Price had so much fun playing bad-guy Ratigan that two extra songs were written specially for him. Look out for a cameo appearance in the toy store from a little wind-up **DUMBO**.

 Star rating: ✪✪✪

The Adventures of Huck Finn
PG
Buena Vista Pictures Distribution, Inc.   1993
VHS

When his father returns to town, Huckleberry Finn fakes his own death and goes on the run with Jim, his supposed "murderer." British viewers' ears will grate at the sound of a fake cockney accent of **MARY POPPINS** proportions, courtesy of the con man who calls himself "the King" (Jason Robards, Jr.). Thanks to the sloppy ending, you might as well ▶▶ from the moment the con men get their come-uppance — nothing quite beats a tarring and feathering. And yes, Huck is a young Elijah Wood, known today as Frodo Baggins in **LORD OF THE RINGS**.

Star rating: ✪✪

The Adventures of Milo and Otis
Columbia Pictures Entertainment   1989
DVD; VHS

Farmyard pets Milo (a cat) and Otis (a dog) begin a great adventure when Milo is swept downstream and Otis sets off to rescue him. Encounters follow with a bear cub, a snake, and chicks, but never any human beings. A great film, especially for the younger viewers. The DVD includes a "Making of."

Star rating: ✪✪✪

Air Bud

PG

Buena Vista Pictures Distribution, Inc.   1997

DVD; VHS

Coldhearted clown Norm Snively abandons his assistant, Buddy the golden retriever, after a performance goes wrong. The outcast dog bumps into lonely boy Josh Framm on a basketball court, where the pair discover Buddy's previously unknown talent for shooting hoops. ⏩ to the basketball matches — Buddy can shoot hoops for real, and it shows on screen! No extras worth speaking of on the DVD.

Star rating: ✪✪✪

Air Bud: Golden Receiver

Miramax Films   1998

DVD; VHS

A few years after **AIR BUD**, Josh is bored with basketball. When he discovers that his mother's new boyfriend is a big fan, he loses interest completely and switches to football. But Bud is a smart dog, and soon learns how to play himself. Doesn't anyone think this is dangerous? Bud returned in yet another sequel, *Air Bud: World Pup*, in which the fickle Josh turns to soccer — impress the adults by claiming to recognize players from the U.S. Women's team, who perform a lot of the fancy footwork. A fourth *Air Bud*, this time the baseball-themed *Seventh Inning Fetch* followed in 2001. What next? Ice-skating?

Star rating: ✪

Aladdin

**Buena Vista Pictures Distribution, Inc.   1992
VHS**

The beautiful princess Jasmine gets tired of being
locked up in the palace and heads out into the
streets in disguise. There she meets poor-boy
Aladdin and his pet monkey, Abu. Aladdin is
thrown in prison by the evil Jafar, but is offered a
chance to escape if he steals a magic lamp from
a dangerous underground cave. The lamp
contains a genie that offers to help him, but can it
also help him become a prince? Beautiful songs,
wonderful animation, a wisecracking genie played
by Robin Williams (see **FLUBBER**), and a very
expressive carpet that never says a word. Annoy
adults by asking: "Is it okay to steal from people
like Aladdin does?"

    Star rating: ✪✪✪✪✪

[Aladdin 2] The Return of Jafar

**Buena Vista Pictures Distribution, Inc.   1994
DVD; VHS**

Jafar, the evil vizier, trapped inside a lamp at the
end of **ALADDIN**, has escaped, and now he has all
the powers of a genie! Although Jafar returns to
menace Aladdin in this straight-to-video sequel,
the funny voice of Robin Williams's genie is
nowhere to be heard. Astound adults by saying
the new genie reminds you of Homer Simpson (it's
the same actor, Dan Castellaneta). Most of these
follow-up "movies" are actually made for video —
though they cost the same to rent, they often seem

to have been made with a lot less care. This is nowhere near as good as **ALADDIN**.

 Star rating: ✪✪

Arabian Night:
ALADDIN
ARABIAN KNIGHT
THE SEVENTH VOYAGE OF SINBAD
THE GOLDEN VOYAGE OF SINBAD

THEME NIGHT

[Aladdin 3] Aladdin and the King of Thieves

Disney Enterprises Inc. 1996
VHS

Aladdin and the Princess Jasmine are finally ready for their wedding. But the preparations are thrown into chaos by the arrival of Cassim and the Forty Thieves, who wish to steal an important magical artifact. Aladdin must begin a new adventure . . . a quest to find the legendary King of Thieves, and his own long-lost father! An unexpected improvement on **THE RETURN OF JAFAR**, perhaps because Robin Williams is back as the genie. A couple of songs, but lots of good fights! Look out, too, for a hidden Mickey Mouse in the opening credits, just before the comet turns yellow — you may need freeze-frame to spot it. Other **ALADDIN** spin-offs include one starring Princess Jasmine and an Aladdin songbook.

 Star rating: ✪✪✪

Alice in Wonderland
Walt Disney Productions/Buena   1951
DVD; VHS

Alice chases the White Rabbit down a rabbit hole and finds herself in the mysterious world of Wonderland. There she meets the Cheshire Cat, whose smile lingers long after he has gone, the Mad Hatter and his fellow diners, and the nonsensical twins Tweedle Dum and Tweedle Dee. Only one of many films based on the classic books by Lewis Carroll, but better known in the world at large for being a Disney production. Little chance for ▶︎ing here — otherwise you might miss tunes like "I'm Late" and the "Unbirthday Song." After you've laughed at the Queen of Hearts's nasty croquet match, the DVD features bonus sing-along versions and the "Making Of" featurette, *Operation Wonderland*.

 Star rating: ✪✪✪

All Dogs Go to Heaven
United Artists Pictures, Inc.   1989
DVD; VHS

Mongrel Charlie escapes from the New Orleans dog pound with his sidekick Itchy. They seek help from their old pal Carface the casino owner, but he swindles them, and Charlie winds up dead. Without any good deeds to boast of in heaven, Charlie tricks his way back down to Earth. The songs aren't very good and the story is too confusing — at times even for adults! ▶▶ after the song "You Can't Keep a Good Dog Down" until the time Charlie escapes from heaven (he's bored there, and you will be, too). After that, things pick up, as the dogs get a pet human who helps them wreak their revenge. The DVD is nothing special.

 Star rating: ✪✪

All Dogs Go to Heaven 2
MGM/UA Distribution Co.   1996
DVD; VHS

Charlie comes back, this time to help a boy on Earth, in a sequel that's actually a little better than the original. It might look cheaper, but the songs are much better (and not flat like in the last film, possibly because Charlie is now played by Charlie Sheen, instead of Burt Reynolds!). But while the film might be an improvement, the DVD is still low on extras. Stump adults by asking how come this takes place in 1996, whereas the original movie took place in 1939. There was also a TV series and the awful *All Dogs Go to Heaven Christmas Carol*.

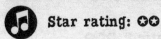 **Star rating: ✪✪**

An American Tail
Universal City Studios, Inc.   1986
VHS

The Mouskewitzes, a family of Russian mice, flee cat persecution by immigrating to America. But young Fievel is washed overboard and arrives alone at the Statue of Liberty. Luckily, he has new friends to help him, including a group of well-dressed French pigeons. America proves to be a land with cats of its own, and the local mice try to find a way to rid themselves of persecution forever. Very young viewers might get scared by the cats.

 Star rating: ✪✪✪

An American Tail: Fievel Goes West
Universal City Studios, Inc.   1991
VHS

You can't keep a good mouse down, and when Cat R. Waul tells the Mouskewitzes of a Western paradise where cats and mice live in harmony, Fievel and family set out in search of it. Just as much fun as the original **AMERICAN TAIL**, perhaps even slightly better. Two further sequels, *The Treasure of Manhattan Island* and *The Mystery of the Night Monster*, are nowhere near as satisfying, but may keep fans entertained.

 Star rating: ✪✪✪

Mouse House:
An American Tail
Mouse Hunt
The Secret of Nimh
The Adventures of the Great
      Mouse Detective

THEME NIGHT

Anastasia

Twentieth Century Fox Film Corp.   1997

DVD; VHS

When they hear of the vast rewards offered by a concerned Empress, con men Dimitri and Vladimir decide to find a girl who can pretend to be the lost princess Anastasia, long presumed dead. They find the perfect candidate in an orphanage, but their "imposter" really *is* Anastasia, who has lost her memory. The proof? Evil sorcerer Rasputin, who wants the whole royal family dead, comes back from the grave to murder her! A mixture of musical, love story, and adventure, ideal for older viewers, although the songs aren't much and Rasputin is *way* too scary for youngsters. The DVD has a couple of sing-alongs and a "Making Of" — better than nothing.

 Star rating: ✪✪✪

[Anastasia 2] Bartok the Magnificent

Twentieth Century Fox Home Entertainment 1999

DVD; VHS

Bartok, Anastasia's plucky bat companion, is drafted to help find Prince Ivan, who has been kidnapped by the witch Baba Yaga. As usual with such sequels, this is much cheaper than the original, but the songs are fun, and the DVD extras include sing-along versions and a maze game you can play on the screen.

 Star rating: ✪✪

Andre

PG
Paramount Pictures Corp.   1994
VHS

In a Maine seaside town, seven-year-old harbormaster's daughter Toni nurses an orphaned baby sea lion back to health. But Andre develops some unique talents, such as a penchant for Hawaiian shirts and some nifty tricks with balls. Dad tries to make him famous, but Andre has human enemies who want him out of the picture for good. Stay for the closing credits — this is based on a true story, and there is footage of the real-life Andre. No fast-forwarding here, but if the caper gets boring, just close your eyes for a while and listen to the 1960s pop music.

 Star rating: ✪✪✪✪

Animalympics

PRD   1979
VHS

A spoof of the Olympics, featuring a load of performing animals! What more do you want? If you liked the soccer game in **BEDKNOBS AND BROOMSTICKS**, then this outdoes it in several wacky set pieces, including hockey, swimming, boxing, diving, and track and field, to name but a few. ⏩ through the slushy rubbish about a dog climbing a mountain and finding a lost paradise — the songs you hear are less interesting than the fun you see. The director Steven Lisberger would go on to make the very different **TRON**.

 Star rating: ✪✪✪

Annie

PG
Columbia Pictures Industries   1982
DVD; VHS

Annie is a poor little orphan girl, tyrannized by the ogre Miss Hannigan. But she wins the chance to visit the wealthy Mr. Warbucks. She soon charms her way into his heart, and he offers a reward if her parents will come to claim her. But Miss Hannigan and her evil associate, Rooster, want the money for themselves! Powerful songs from great singers, but at over two hours this is really, really long. Before long, you'll be hitting ▶every time someone isn't singing. Nothing special on the DVD. Impress adults by telling them that **ANNIE** started life as a comic strip in the 1930s.

 Star rating: ✪✪✪

Antz

PG
DreamWorks Distribution L.L.C.   1998
DVD; VHS

Humble worker-ant Z falls in love with a lady-ant at a dance, only to discover she is the Queen's daughter, Princess Bala. He joins the army to impress her and is hailed as a hero when he accidentally survives a battle with termites. But soldier-ant General Mandible plans on leading a revolution, and only Z can stop him. Plenty of icky insects, with grown-up gags hiding in the background to keep the parents entertained — as well as top stars Woody Allen and Sylvester Stallone doing voice-overs. Lots of extras on the DVD, but they're mainly for grown-ups.

 Star rating: ✪✪✪✪

Arabian Knight
Miramax Films   1995
VHS

A thief steals magic items from the Sultan's palace, and Princess Yumyum must go on a quest, escorted by Tac the shy cobbler, to seek the help of a mysterious witch. A very strange film — parts of it were made 20 years before other parts of it, the thief and the cobbler were originally supposed to be completely mute, and a load of songs were added after the original director was fired. Despite this troubled past, an excellent film for all the family. But just imagine how much better it could have been without too many cooks spoiling the broth.

    Star rating: ✪✪✪✪

The Aristocats
Walt Disney Productions/Buena   1970
DVD; VHS

The aging Madame Bonfamille decides to leave all her wealth to her beloved cats, but her scheming butler has ideas of his own. He abandons Duchess the cat and her three adorable kittens in the country, but they find their way back home with the help of lovable rogue alley cat O'Malley. Some swinging songs here, and a simple story even the young ones can enjoy — but once they meet O'Malley, you can ⏩ through their journey back to Paris. The good stuff starts once they're back home, and the two British geese they meet on the way are just irritating.

   Star rating: ✪✪✪

Asterix the Gaul
Extrafilm   1967
VHS

All of Gaul has been conquered by the Roman
Empire. All? No, not all. One small village of
indomitable locals holds out against the invaders.
There are six other cartoons in the series, including
Asterix and the Big Fight, *The Twelve Tasks of
Asterix*, *Asterix and Cleopatra*, and *Asterix vs.
Caesar*. But not all are available in English, and
you're better off sticking to the original comic
books.

Star rating: ✪✪

Asterix (5) in Britain
Extrafilm   1986
VHS

In 50 B.C., the Romans invade Britain, and one
village sends to Gaul for help. Asterix, Obelix, and
Getafix take along their magic potion . . . and
there's a big fight, as usual in the **ASTERIX** films. This
video is only available in the United Kingdom, but
keep an eye out for it on TV.

Star rating: ✪✪

Asterix (7) Conquers America
Extrafilm   1994
VHS

The Romans have had enough of the meddling
Druid Getafix and his magic potion. They decide to
throw him off the edge of the world, but instead he
lands in a formerly unknown land — America. Asterix
and Obelix go in search of him, eventually returning

to find that, while they were away, the Romans have conquered their village and enslaved their friends. Better known in America than the other *Asterix* films, for obvious reasons. 🕒 to Asterix's boat on the high seas — the storm scene used 40 camera angles and 5,000 hours of computer time to make, so you might as well get your money's worth.

Star rating: ☺☺

Asterix and Obelix Take on Caesar
PG
Pathé   1999
DVD; VHS

Dastardly Roman general Detritus uses the druid Getafix's magic potion to seize power. Julius Caesar becomes his prisoner, and Obelix becomes his bodyguard! It's up to Asterix to save the day, in a live-action movie of the famous comics — though, like **THE FLINTSTONES**, it makes you wonder what the point is of trying to copy a cartoon with real people. Originally made in French, which is why nobody's mouth seems to match what they are saying. Impress adults by noticing that Obelix (Gérard Depardieu) also appeared as the fashion victim Le Pelt in **102 DALMATIANS**. Nothing special on the DVD.

Star rating: ☺☺

Atlantis: The Lost Empire
PG
Buena Vista Pictures Distribution, Inc.   2001
VHS

Milo Thatch (played by **BACK TO THE FUTURE**'s Michael J. Fox), goes in search of the lost city of Atlantis, but when he eventually finds it, it is a dying culture, threatened by bad guys from the surface world. Milo needs to help the Atlanteans read the ancient runes to save their world — with time out for a fabulous fight with a giant robot sea creature. Annoy adults by asking: "If Princess Kida can remember the olden days, how come she's forgotten how to read?" Suspiciously similar to *Nadia: The Secret of Blue Water* — a Japanese cartoon also available in the United States.

Star rating: ✪✪✪✪

Babar: King of the Elephants
HBO Home Video   1999
DVD; VHS

Little elephant Babar is all alone when his mother is killed. He stumbles into the city, where he is adopted by the kindly Madame, who teaches him how to read, how to drive, and how to serve tea. Eventually, his friends Celeste and Arthur take him back to the forest, where he must overthrow the evil rhinos. There was also a *Babar* TV series, some episodes of which made their way into video stores. One episode is also included on the DVD as a bonus, which is better than nothing. Right now, **BABAR** is only available in the United Kingdom, but it may come to the United States soon. Until then, watch for it on TV.

Star rating: ✪

★★★★★★★★★★★★★★★★★★★★★★★★★★★★★★★★★★★★
★ **Credit watching:** Even child actors have
★ to go to school for a minimum number of
★ hours every day. That's why some credits
★ list a "Studio Teacher."
★★★★★★★★★★★★★★★★★★★★★★★★★★★★★★★★★★★★

Babe

Universal City Studios, Inc.   1995

DVD; VHS

Babe the piglet is won as a prize by the kindly Farmer Hoggett. Befriending all the animals on the farm, including even the sheep and sheepdogs, Babe learns that the humans intend to eat him for Christmas dinner. He decides to make himself useful as a sheep-pig — herding the animals in place of the farmer's old dog Rex. One of the best-ever films for kids (and great fun for adults, too), from the singing mice to the proclamation that "Christmas means carnage!" Babe himself was played by 48 different piglets, each trained to perform a specific task. The DVD version includes only "Scene Access" as an extra. Is that the best they could do?

 Star rating: ✪✪✪✪✪

Babe — Pig in the City

Universal City Studios, Inc.   1998

DVD; VHS

After Farmer Hoggett has an accident, Mrs. Hoggett takes Babe to a fair in the Big City (see if you can guess where it's supposed to be — it seems to contain the Statue of Liberty, the Eiffel Tower, *and* the Sydney Opera House). But when Mrs. Hoggett is arrested, Babe is left alone and must evade the city's evil animal-catchers. A very dark and disappointing sequel to the original — not at all what you're probably expecting and best avoided. Not much but animated menus and a screensaver on the DVD. That *won't* do, Pig.

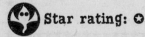 **Star rating: ✪**

Although FAIRY TALE ... A TRUE STORY was based on real events in 1917, 70 years later, the girls involved admitted that they faked their fairy pictures. So it's not really a "true" story after all.

Back to the Future
PG
Universal City Studios, Inc.   1985
VHS

Teenager Marty McFly accidentally goes back in time to 1955 and meets his parents when they were still at school. Now he has to get them to fall in love, or he will never be born! Not quite a film for *all* the family — very young kids will get bored by jokes they don't understand and occasional kissing stuff. But watch out for the incredible skateboard chase around the town square and the don't-try-this-at-home antics of mad Doc Brown in a thunderstorm. Funny how time flies . . . back in *1985*, *your* parents were probably Marty's age!

 Star rating: ✪✪✪✪

Back to the Future Part II
PG
Universal City Studios, Inc.   1989
VHS

Doc Brown, inventor of the time machine, takes Marty to the future year of 2015 to help his own children out of trouble — watch out for a replay of the first film's skateboard sequence, but this time on hover-boards! But town bully Biff steals a book that allows him to change history. Now Marty has to jump back to 1955 again, to stop Biff from messing up the past. No DVD available . . . how old-fashioned!

 Star rating: ✪✪✪

Back to the Future Part III
PG
Universal City Studios, Inc.   1990
VHS

The explosive finale to the **BACK TO THE FUTURE** trilogy, with Marty sent back to his town's early days in the Wild West of 1885. But this time, it's the Doc who is in trouble — he's fallen in love with a woman who shouldn't even be alive! An entertaining mix of comedy, cowboy movie, and sci-fi, and like all the other films in the series, one which rewards repeat viewings. Look out for the band at the town dance — it's heavy rockers ZZ Top. The finale introduces the Doc's children, Jules and Verne, who are also featured in the later animated TV series.

 Star rating: ✪✪✪✪

Balto
Universal City Studios, Inc.   1995
VHS

In 1925, the remote town of Nome, Alaska, is struck by a terrible disease. The only way to save the townspeople is to get the serum to them by dogsled, across the snowy wastes. The pedigreed dog Steele prepares to lead the team that will pull the humans' sled, but it's half-wolf Balto who really saves the day. Based on a true story, but sometimes truth can do with a little editing — this just seems to go on and on. Also followed by the typically lackluster sequel, *Balto II: Wolf Quest*. There is a statue of the real-life Balto in New York's Central Park.

Star rating: ✪✪✪

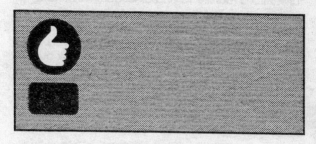

Bambi

**Walt Disney Productions/Buena   1942
VHS**

Bambi the baby deer befriends Thumper the rabbit and Flower the skunk. His mother warns him to be wary of the creature known as Man, but she is killed by a hunter. Bambi grows up and falls in love with Faline the doe, but the forest is threatened by a fire, and he must save the animals. A wonderful film, but there's no avoiding it — it contains heartrending moments that can easily cause distress and nightmares in soft-hearted individuals. Embarrass adults by tugging at their sleeve and asking: "Daddy, are you crying?" You'll know when, because you will be, too. Hunting-savvy viewers might also wonder how Bambi's mother gets shot in spring, when hunting season starts in the autumn. No DVD release, which is simply foolish.

    Star rating: ✪✪✪✪✪

Barney's Great Adventure
Polygram Films   1998
DVD; VHS

Cody, Abby, and Marcella are sent to stay on their grandparents' farm, where Barney the cuddly toy turns into a real-life talking dinosaur. They find a rainbow egg, but must return it to its place of origin, in a musical quest through the local town guaranteed to appeal to very young viewers. Older audience members might like to look out for the marching band scene (everyone has long shadows one minute, and then none the next) but would probably rather find something better to do. The DVD includes *Barney's First Adventure* as an extra.

Star rating: ✪✪✪

*batteries not included
PG
Universal City Studios, Inc.   1987
DVD; VHS

Frank and Faye, an old couple living in a condemned New York apartment building, pray for a miracle. They get more than they bargained for when their building is invaded by kindly miniature UFOs, whose occupants can also fix any kind of broken machinery. With old-timers in the lead roles, this even has something to keep the grandparents happy. A few scraps on the DVD, but nothing special.

 Star rating: ✪✪✪

Beauty and the Beast

Buena Vista Pictures Distribution, Inc.   1991
DVD; VHS

Belle goes in search of her father when he gets lost in a dark forest. He has been imprisoned in a castle by The Beast, a prince who has been transformed into an ugly creature by a curse. The Beast says he will let Belle's father leave, but only if she promises to stay herself . . . FOREVER! A great fairy-tale cartoon, with lovable characters and great songs (listen out for "Be Our Guest," which was nominated for an Oscar, or "Beauty and the Beast," which won one). Watch for muscle-bound poser Gaston (who wants Belle for himself), and dancing household items, including the French-waiter candelabra. Impress the adults by saying "That talking teapot sounds like the witch in **BEDKNOBS AND BROOMSTICKS**." (Same actress, Angela Lansbury.) Look out for plenty of hidden Mickey Mouses, in wood carvings, by the door frame, and in the winding knob at the back of Cogsworth's head. Poor sequels include *Belle's Magical World*, the terrible *Beauty and the Beast: Enchanted Christmas*, and the TV series *Sing Me a Story with Belle*. Stick to the original.

 Star rating: ✪✪✪✪

 CASPER might be a ghost, but making him as a digital effect took up 29 trillion bytes of computer power.

Bedknobs and Broomsticks
Walt Disney Productions/Buena   **1971**
DVD; VHS

In wartime England, three kids are sent to stay with a lady who lives by the sea. She is a trainee witch who plans to use magic against enemy invaders, and she whisks the children off on a flying bed, where they find themselves in magical lands inhabited by cartoon characters like those in **MARY POPPINS**. Watch out for the animal soccer match and a dance number in London's antique market Portobello Road. But much of the story is taken up with the "search" for a magical item, which turns out to be where one of the children said it would be all along. Many people will want to 🅿️ after the flying bed scene straight to the cartoon soccer match. Annoy adults by pointing out: "If grown-ups just listened to what kids told them, this film would be a lot shorter."

 Star rating: ✪✪✪

Beethoven
Universal City Studios, Inc.   **1991**
DVD; VHS

Canine comedy about a dog-hating dad, George Newton, stuck with a cute little Saint Bernard puppy that soon grows into a giant disaster area! Smashing of dishes, biting of sensitive parts, and all-round chaos ensue. Beethoven is on the run from evil vet Dr. Harmick — impress the adults by noticing that the same actor was a good guy in the **THE LOVE BUG** (Dean Jones). And for *X-Files* fans, look out for David Duchovny (Mulder) as a slimy yuppie. Sharp observers might ask themselves:

"What kind of alarm system has lasers, but doesn't notice when you shower it with broken glass?"

Star rating: ❂❂❂

LITE Night:
DOCTOR DOLITTLE
BEETHOVEN
MRS. DOUBTFIRE
HOME ALONE

THEME NIGHT

Beethoven's 2nd
PG
Universal City Studios, Inc.   1993
DVD; VHS

Just as funny as the first movie, except that now Beethoven is a dad, too. He falls in love with a female Saint Bernard (a Saint Bernadette?) called Sissy, but her evil owner Regina wants her back. She also wants to sell the couple's four adorable puppies, which have to be kept hidden. Six Saint Bernards might not be quite as chaotic as **101 DALMATIONS**, but they certainly give it a good try. Watch out for Beethoven pulling the side off a house to rescue Ryce Newton from a boy intent on Unwelcome Kissing Stuff. Also watch the girl whose tickets Beethoven retrieves from a bully — she starts off with her hair in a ponytail, which then disappears!

Star rating: ❂❂❂

Beethoven's 3rd

Universal Studios Home Video, Inc.   2000

DVD; VHS

Beethoven is supposed to head across America in his "uncle" Richard's mobile home, but "auntie" Beth has him locked in a kennel. Of course, the resourceful dog escapes and catches up with them, but they are being chased by bad guys who want to steal a valuable computer program. Nowhere near as good as **BEETHOVEN** or **BEETHOVEN'S 2ND**, but watch out for Beethoven's meeting with a skunk, and an important lesson for boys who have a secret love of Hello Kitty. ◗◗ whenever the dog isn't on-screen — which is quite often. Yet another sequel, *Beethoven's 4th*, followed in 2001 and featured the dog sent away to obedience school and accidentally swapped with an evil twin.

Star rating: ✪✪

Big

PG

Twentieth Century Fox Film Corp.   1988

DVD; VHS

Teenager Josh Baskin wishes he were bigger, and does so in front of a magic fortune-telling machine that turns him into a 35-year-old man. With a child's brain in an adult's body, he does the logical thing and gets a job at a toy company, testing the latest inventions. A modern update of the **FREAKY FRIDAY** concept — ◗◗ to the toy store scene where Josh plays "Chopsticks" on a giant piano. The DVD extra list could do with being . . . bigger.

 Star rating: ✪✪✪

Black Beauty

Paramount Pictures Corp.   1971
DVD; VHS

A horse tells the story of its life and various owners
in a charming film of the classic children's book.
One for almost all the family, though younger
viewers may be disturbed by the scene in the
burning barn, and Beauty does undergo some
harrowing treatment before he gets the loving
owner he deserves. Nothing extra on the DVD,
which doesn't make horse sense. There is also a
more recent animated version.

Star rating: ✪✪✪✪

The Black Cauldron

PG
Walt Disney Productions/Buena   1985
DVD; VHS

Warrior Taran, helped by princess Eilonwy and Hen
Wen the sorcerous pig, must keep the magical
cauldron out of the hands of the evil Horned King,
otherwise civilization itself will fall apart. Not your
typical Disney cartoon — much darker and scarier,
with a distinct lack of singing animals, this was the
first Disney cartoon to get a PG rating. Not your
typical Disney DVD either — it has a bonus *Donald
Duck* short, a trivia game, and a gallery of artwork.

Star rating: ✪✪✪

The Black Hole

PG

Walt Disney Productions/Buena   1979

VHS

A group of astronauts in search of the long-lost ship *Cygnus* find it held by a force field at the brink of a black hole. But Captain Reinhardt has gone mad and turned his crew into robots, and now he wants them all to accompany him on a one-way trip into the black hole. Unless you care about robot V.I.N.CENT wandering around the ship, you can ⏩ to where the laser guns start shooting. A rip-off of **STAR WARS**, but since this is from the Disney company, it still has in-jokes. Bad super-robot Maximilian is modeled on the devil from **FANTASIA**.

Star rating: ✪✪

The Black Stallion

United Artists   1979

DVD; VHS

Young boy Alec is shipwrecked on a desert island, along with Black, the magnificent horse he befriended onboard the ship. Later, the pair are rescued and brought back to America, where Alec decides to become a jockey. The horse is stolen by Arabs in the sequel, called *The Black Stallion Returns*, so you can probably guess what happens.

Star rating: ✪✪✪✪

BMX Bandits
PG

Comworld Pictures   1984

BMX-loving boys Goose and P.J. fool around in the supermarket, and fellow biker Judy loses her job as a result. Hanging around at the lake, the trio find some short-wave radios and discover that crooks are planning to use them in a bank robbery. BMX stands for Bicycle Motocross, which might have meant something to *your* parents. This is how weird **POKÉMON** is going to look to *your* kids. A very old, very silly Australian film, likely only to appeal to people who like bikes. ▶ to the chases, which feature professional stunt-cyclists standing in for the actors. This isn't available in the United States, but that's no big loss.

Star rating: ✪

The Borrowers
PG

Polygram Filmed Entertainment   1997
VHS

The Clock family are "borrowers" — tiny people the size of mice, befriended by full-size human boy Pete Lender. They have to team up to save their house from nasty lawyer Ocious C. Potter, but not before high adventure in the kitchen, a brush with Jêff the Exterminator, and a trek across town for a fight in a dairy. Some strange similarities with the house-moving sequence in **TOY STORY**. Annoy adults by asking: "Why does Ocious send a man to squish the Borrowers? Why doesn't he just demolish the house?" There was also a *Borrowers* TV series.

Star rating: ✪✪

A Bug's Life

Buena Vista Pictures Distribution, Inc.   1998
DVD; VHS

Flik the ant and his humble anthill buddies are pressed into slavery by Hopper and his gang of ruthless grasshoppers. With the whole hill in danger, Flik promises to recruit a group of warriors to save them, but the best he can do is a group of out-of-luck circus performers, including a fat caterpillar, a ladybug that ain't no lady, and some performing pillbugs. Just an antenna ahead of **ANTZ** in the race to be "Best Bug Movie" of the 1990s. Loaded with references to other films, including Pizza Planet (from **TOY STORY**). Also listen for the two flies that can't "stay out of the light" — they are John Lasseter and Andrew Stanton, who directed the film! The DVD includes a set of joke "bloopers."

 Star rating: ✪✪✪✪✪

Bugsy Malone

Paramount Pictures Corp.   1976
VHS

A tough gangster movie, but with all the parts played by kids, with some fabulous songs and absolutely gallons of custard-pie fights. Look out for a young Michael Jackson playing the piano and a young Jodie Foster as a gangster's moll. Guaranteed to satisfy the greatest food-fight urges, without messing up your own kitchen. Scare adults by asking if you can have custard for dinner.

 Star rating: ✪✪

Candleshoe

Walt Disney Productions/Buena   1977
DVD; VHS

Priory the faithful butler becomes a master of
disguise to convince his wealthy employer that life
has not changed in England. But he also wants to
find lost treasure so that her home does not have
to be sold. For that he will need the help of some
local ne'er-do-wells and Casey, a young American
impostor. Strangely similar to **ANNIE**, and featuring
Jodie Foster from **BUGSY MALONE** as the plucky
Casey. Nothing at all on the DVD, though the
leaflet in the box helpfully gives away most of the
plot.

Star rating: ✪✪✪

Casper

PG
Universal City Studios, Inc.   1995
VHS

Greedy heiress Carrigan Crittenden inherits a
house, haunted by the repulsive ghosts Stretch,
Stinkie, and Fatso. Dr. Harvey and daughter, Kat,
are hired to banish the ghosts, but Kat befriends a
fourth ghost, little Casper. A great mixture of
comedy, tragedy, and ghost busting, featuring
an animated Casper amid real, live people. Count
the number of times an extremely dangerous act
(such as playing with a blender) is presented as
harmless — pretty dangerous! Followed by
Casper's Haunted Christmas.

Star rating: ✪✪✪

The Cat from Outer Space

Walt Disney Productions/Buena   1978

DVD; VHS

Zunar J5/90 Doric 4-7 (or Jake, for short) is an alien whose spaceship crash-lands in America. And he's a cat. He needs gold to repair it, but a crook wants Jake's diamond necklace for himself. Jake enlists the help of a local boy, who must also keep him hidden from government alien hunters. Close encounters of the furred kind, and remarkably similar in premise to the later my-dog's-an-alien movie **Lilo and Stitch**.

Star rating: ✪✪

★★★★★★★★★★★★★★★★★★★★★★★★★★★★★★★★★★★
★   ★
★   **Credit watching:** A "Gaffer" is the chief   ★
★   electrician.   ★
★   ★
★★★★★★★★★★★★★★★★★★★★★★★★★★★★★★★★★★★

Catnapped!

Pioneer   1995

DVD; VHS

Toriyasu and his sister, Miko, are transported to the magical world of Banipal Witt, where they are transformed into cats. Toriyasu's dog Papadoll has become a henchman of the witch-queen Bubulina, and they have three days to rescue him before they all turn into monsters. A surreal and dreamy cartoon adventure — though while the animation may be state-of-the-art, the DVD extras are disappointing, limited to little more than character bios.

 Star rating: ✪✪✪

Cats & Dogs

PG

Warner Bros.   2001

DVD; VHS

"It is you who is in trouble, baby puppy." Lou (a beagle) is an inexperienced dog-agent, accidentally assigned to protect a professor working on a serum to cure allergy to dogs. But evil cat-mastermind Mr. Tinkles plans to steal the serum and alter it, creating a virus that will make everyone allergic to dogs and make cats the rulers of the world. Done with real people and clever animal-tronics. ▶▶ to the ninja Siamese cats — they know kung fu.

 Star rating: ✪✪✪

Cats Don't Dance

Warner Bros.   1997

VHS

Young kitten Danny comes to Hollywood in search of a musical career, but makes a new enemy in the shape of Darla Dimple, a bratty human child-star who hates animals. Catchy tunes, including "Nothing's Gonna Stop Us" and slapstick action like the old-school Warner Brothers toons.

 Star rating: ✪✪✪

Charlotte's Web

Paramount Pictures Corp.   1973

DVD; VHS

Wilbur is a baby pig, raised as a pet by a farmer, but sold to another farm. Charlotte the spider knows Wilbur will be killed and eaten, so uses her web-spinning skills to convince the local people that Wilbur can work miracles. Nice songs and a sweet story, but it's no match for **BABE**. The DVD has a "Meet the Animals" guessing game.

 Star rating: ✪✪✪

Chicken Run

DreamWorks Distribution L.L.C.   2000

DVD; VHS

A group of hens plot to escape from the egg farm, where they are kept prisoner by the evil Tweedys. Newcomer rooster Rocky pretends he can teach them to fly, but won't admit that he can't fly, either. He used to be shot from a circus cannon! Then the Tweedys decide to go into chicken pie making, and the race is on to save the hens from a horrible end. No fast-forwarding here; every moment is a treat. A fabulously funny feathery feature from the makers of **WALLACE AND GROMIT**. Lots of extras on the DVD, including a read-along, games, and "Making of" featurettes.

 Star rating: ✪✪✪✪✪

 The name "FINAL FANTASY" came about because the original game was the company's last chance to succeed before it ran out of money. But it was so successful that there have now been ten "Final" Fantasy games, as well as the FF: SPIRITS WITHIN movie.

Chitty Chitty Bang Bang
United Artists   1968
DVD; VHS

Inventor Professor Potts repairs and improves an old car so it can fly. Accompanied by his children, Jeremy and Jemima, and a lady called Truly Scrumptious, they fly on a rescue mission to a castle in Vulgaria, where children are NOT ALLOWED. Wonderful, singable songs, but you may want to hide behind the sofa when the Child Catcher arrives — that goes for the adults, too! Watch out for Jeremy's hair during the song "Hushabye Mountain," it seems to comb itself. At two and a half hours, this may be too long for restless viewers. Script by Roald Dahl.

  Star rating: ✪✪✪✪

A Christmas Carol

PRD   1951

DVD; VHS

Scrooge the miser changes his ways after a visit from three ghosts. You know the rest, and so, it would seem, do all the film companies who constantly churn out remakes and alterations of the Charles Dickens classic. Grandparents will prefer the 1950s version with Alastair Sim, while a more recent 1990s film stars Patrick Stewart (*Star Trek*'s Captain Picard) as Scrooge. The middle ground in the 1980s is the one with George C. Scott.

Star rating: ✪✪✪

Cinderella

Walt Disney Productions/Buena   1949

VHS

Cinderella is persecuted by her stepmother and two ugly stepsisters, but the fairy godmother ensures that she does go to the ball and meet her handsome Prince Charming. That's the famous fairy tale, but this version adds plenty of cartoon animals in typical Disney style — including the memorable mice Jacques and Gus-Gus and Lucifer the evil cat. ▶ to "Bibbidy-Bobbidi-Boo," a magical song that was nominated for an Oscar. There was also a *Cinderella* cartoon series in Japan, which added attacking pirates and a prince who was an impostor!

 Star rating: ✪✪✪✪

Clash of the Titans

PG

MGM Film Company   1981

VHS

Perseus, the son of Zeus, falls in love with Andromeda, a princess who is due to be sacrificed to the Kraken sea monster. He has just thirty days to find a way to defeat it. After the destruction of Argos (a city drowned by the Kraken), ⏩ to Perseus's terrifying battle with Medusa and the fight with the scorpions. Great fun for all the family, from the people who brought you **JASON AND THE ARGONAUTS**.

 Star rating: ✪✪✪☆

Greek Week:

HERCULES

JASON AND THE ARGONAUTS

CLASH OF THE TITANS

THEME NIGHT

Condorman

PG

Walt Disney Productions/Buena   1981

DVD; VHS

Natalia, a defecting Russian spy, mistakes comic artist Woody for a CIA agent and asks him to help her. Woody jumps at the chance to turn his comic ideas into reality — including a super-powered boat, a transforming car, and a flying suit. ⏩ to the arrival of each gadget — the high point has to be the car chase, which wrecks a lifetime's supply of Porsches on a winding European road. No extras on the DVD.

Star rating: ✪✪✪

Courage Mountain
PG
Epic Productions, Inc.   1989
VHS

Fourteen-year-old Heidi is sent to Italy by her grandfather, but her school is commandeered for the war effort (it's 1915). Heidi and her friends are forced to work in an orphanage, but the plucky girl decides they should escape and flee back to her native Alps. And if that sounds remotely familiar, that's because this is a sequel to the popular Heidi story, retold in many films and the famous TV series. Featuring a young Charlie Sheen as Heidi's would-be boyfriend Peter.

Star rating: ✪✪✪

D.A.R.Y.L.
PG
Paramount Pictures Corp.   1985
VHS

Daryl is the new kid at the foster home, but then his real "parents" come looking for him. They are scientists, and he is really D.A.R.Y.L., a Data Analyzing Robot Youth Life-form. After the explosive opening sequence, ⏩ to the second half, when Daryl's robot powers start to make things a lot more interesting.

Star rating: ✪✪

Danny the Champion of the World
Walt Disney Productions/Wonderworks et al.
1989
VHS

Nine-year-old Danny lives in a trailer with his widowed father. But the evil landlord Hazell wants them to leave their land so he can build a housing development. They decide to go back, using all their poaching expertise to trap the crooks, in an ecological adventure from famous children's author Roald Dahl. Watch for the realistic way Dad and Danny interact with each other — they are played by real-life father and son Jeremy and Samuel Irons. This British flick hasn't been released yet in the United States, but may show up on a TV screen near you.

Star rating: ✪✪✪

Darby O'Gill and the Little People
Walt Disney Productions/Buena   1969
VHS

Caretaker Darby falls down a well in Ireland, where he discovers the land of the leprechauns. He gets three wishes . . . but how will he use them? If you had three wishes, you'd probably ask for something a little more modern than this antique Disney, but ▶ to the fiery banshee sequence,

****
★ **Credit watching:** A "Wrangler" is the person ★
★ on the set who looks after any animals ★
★ needed for the film. ★
****

43

and look out for a very young Sean Connery as
Michael McBride.

Star rating: ✪✪

The Dark Crystal
PG
Universal City Studios, Inc.   1982
DVD; VHS

Jen and Kira, the last survivors of the Gelfling race,
must restore the missing shard to the Dark Crystal,
or the evil Skeksis creatures will rule the world. A
very serious fantasy adventure using the same
puppetry techniques as THE MUPPET MOVIE, far too
scary (and slow) for the very young, but a delight
for older viewers. Watch for the cosmic balance
between the bad Skeksis and good Mystics — who
are two halves of the same soul . . . very deep. The
DVD features many deleted scenes and a "Making
of" documentary.

 Star rating: ✪✪✪

Dennis the Menace
Trimark Pictures   1993
DVD; VHS

Six-year-old Dennis must stay with his grouchy
neighbor Mr. Wilson while his parents are away.
Sam the thief breaks into Mr. Wilson's house to steal
his coin collection, but kidnaps Dennis. But a young
rascal like Dennis is too much for his captor. A
slapstick comedy in the tradition of HOME ALONE.
There was also a disappointing video sequel,
Dennis the Menace Strikes Again.

Star rating: ✪✪

44

Dexter's Laboratory: Ego Trip

Cartoon Network   1998

VHS

Child-scientist Dexter is surprised by the arrival of time-traveling robot assassins, who have come to stop someone from saving the future. Immediately assuming they mean him, Dexter sets off on a trip through time to meet three very different versions of himself. Great fun for anyone who loved **BACK TO THE FUTURE**.

Star rating: ✪✪✪✪

Digby, the Biggest Dog in the World

Cinerama Releasing   1974

DVD; VHS

Digby the sheepdog accidentally eats a chemical designed to increase the size of food grown in space. He expands to giant proportions, and the race is on to shrink him before the army blows him to bits. ◖ whenever the giant dog isn't causing havoc on screen, which is disappointingly often.

Star rating: ✪✪

THEME NIGHT

Height Night:
DIGBY, THE BIGGEST DOG IN THE WORLD
HONEY, I BLEW UP THE KID
BIG
CLASH OF THE TITANS

Digimon: The Movie
Twentieth Century Fox Film Corp.   2000
DVD; VHS

Young Kari finds an egg growing in her father's computer screen, which hatches into a Digital Monster. It is just one of several kindly creatures that are threatened by bad creatures such as the Diaboromon, which turns up four years later. Then they fight. Then there's another fight. This movie is a mess because it's not a movie at all — it's three short "specials" glued together.

Star rating: ☻

Dinosaur
PG
Buena Vista Pictures Distribution, Inc.   2000
DVD; VHS

On prehistoric Earth, a family of monkeylike lemurs finds Aladar, an orphaned baby dinosaur. They raise him as their own, and the full-grown lizard leads them to safety when their former home is destroyed by a meteorite. The family joins a herd of dinosaurs in search of the paradise of "the Nesting Grounds," and a tough trek across the desert ensues, harried by predators and bullied by the dinosaur leader Kron. ◗ through the whole trek cross the desert. They walk . . . they moan . . . they walk . . . they moan. If you've seen **THE LAND BEFORE TIME** movies, the story may seem strangely familiar, and if you want dinosaurs that talk (but don't sing), you're in for a treat. But this is too scary for younger kids, while older ones will wonder why they shouldn't just watch **JURASSIC PARK** again.

Star rating: ☻☻

The ADDAMS FAMILY is named after Charles Addams, the cartoonist who originally created the characters for the *New Yorker* magazine.

Doctor Dolittle
Foxvideo Inc.   1967
VHS

Doctor Dolittle finds that he can talk (and sing) to animals, and that they talk back. He sets off in search of a Pink Sea Snail and a Giant Lunar Moth, in this very long and somewhat tiresome musical, which stars more than 1,500 real-life animals.
⏩ from song to song — or use only as "one last thing" to watch before bedtime, thus allowing you to stay up for another two and a half hours.

   Star rating: ✪

Doctor Dolittle
PG-13
Twentieth Century Fox Film Corp.   1998
DVD; VHS

A very different, modernized version of the famous story, featuring Eddie Murphy as John Dolittle, an adult doctor who has forgotten that as a child he used to "talk to the animals." But his memory is jolted, and soon he's surrounded by a menagerie of wisecracking, argumentative, farting animals. Not one to watch with the grandparents . . . they will probably be scandalized by all the parts you find hilarious. Watch for the circus sequence when

47

John visits the sick tiger. Wandering in the background you can see a Push-me Pull-you creature from the original movie. Murphy returned a couple of years later with the *slightly* tamer *Doctor Dolittle II*, in which he must help the animals in a forest protect their domain from lumberjacks.

Star rating: ✪✪✪

A Dog of Flanders
PG
Warner Bros.   1998
DVD; VHS

Nello and his grandfather find an injured dog and nurse it back to health, calling it Patraasche after Nello's mother. Nello is fascinated by art and befriends Alois, a girl with similar interests. But tragedy soon sets in. It's one of the weepiest stories since **OLD YELLER** and not for the fainthearted. This famous European tale has been adapted into a film many times — there is also a Japanese animated version available in the United States. Like many Hollywood remakes, this version tacks on a happy ending, but it's still a tearful tale of a boy and his dog. Astound adults by informing them that Flanders is the part of Belgium where people still speak a dialect of Dutch (Flemish).

Star rating: ✪✪✪

Dougal and the Blue Cat
PRD   1970
VHS

Dougal the sugar-lump-loving dog is perplexed by the arrival of Buxton, a blue cat, in the magic garden. Soon Zebedee's mustache disappears, Dougal's friends are imprisoned, and Dougal himself is banished to the Moon. This British film is very weird indeed, but all the more fun for it. Adults will love being reminded of their own childhoods, while the very young will just watch the colors.

 Star rating: ☺☺☺

Doug's 1st Movie
Buena Vista Pictures Distribution, Inc.   1999
VHS

Evil industrialist Bluff has dumped some evil waste materials into Lucky Duck Lake and accidentally created a mutant monster. Local boy Doug, however, befriends the monster and calls him Herman Melville. To impress local girl Patti Mayonnaise, Doug intends to help Herman escape, but first he will have to foil Bluff's men, who are intent on killing Herman to protect their boss's business.

Star rating: ☺☺

Dragonheart
PG-13
Universal City Studios, Inc.   1996
DVD; VHS

Realizing he would be out of a job with no dragons to slay, Bowen the knight joins forces with Draco, the last dragon on Earth. The pair dupe villagers into believing that only Bowen can save them, until he and Draco are called to save the land from its evil king. Watch for Gilbert's archery lesson — the feathers on his second arrow lose their spots as he lifts it to take aim. Loaded with DVD extras, though like the film itself, these are more suitable for older viewers. Scare your parents by saying: "A.D. 948? England didn't have a King Einon in A.D. 948! It was Edmund I."

Star rating: ✪✪✪

Dragonslayer
PG
Paramount Pictures Corp.   1981
VHS

King Ulrich keeps a marauding dragon away from his kingdom by regularly sacrificing maidens to it. But when the next sacrifice is the king's own daughter, a wizard and his young apprentice take matters into their own hands. A dark, forbidding scary-fairy tale, with bloodthirsty sequences likely to have the younger ones hiding behind the sofa. Not your average Disney film at all, and all the better for it.

 Star rating: ✪✪✪

Dumbo
Walt Disney Productions/Buena   1941
DVD; VHS

Dumbo the baby elephant is the laughingstock of the circus, until, thanks to some local crows and his friend Timothy the mouse, he discovers that he can fly. ⚫ to the "Pink Elephants on Parade" sequence. The song "Baby Mine" won an Oscar, as did the film's music. Many years later, it was followed by the TV series *Dumbo's Circus*. The 60th anniversary DVD is absolutely dripping with extras, including bonus short cartoons, a storybook section, sing-along songs, a commentary, and art gallery.

  Star rating: ✪✪✪✪

Dunston Checks In
PG
Twentieth Century Fox Film Corp.   **1995**
VHS

Dunston the orangutan is smuggled into the Majestic Hotel to steal valuables for the evil Lord Rutledge. But he escapes, befriends the sons of the hotel owner, and soon causes utter chaos — much to the annoyance of animal catchers and hotel inspectors. A hilarious monkey movie, and fun for all the family.

 Star rating: ✪✪✪

The Emperor's New Groove
Buena Vista Pictures Distribution, Inc.   **2000**
DVD; VHS

Central American Emperor Kuzco is transformed into a llama by Yzma the witch. He resolves to regain his throne, but the only person who can help him is Pacha, whose village he is threatening to demolish to make way for a swimming pool. An Aztec buddy-movie, featuring a fat peasant and a bad-tempered pack animal (think of it as THE ROAD TO EL DORADO meets SHREK!). As with other more recent Disney films, released in two DVD editions — the 2 Disc "ultimate" set is dripping with extras, but even the standard version contains plenty to justify the extra expense, including a trivia game, game demos, and music videos.

 Star rating: ❂❂❂

Escape to Witch Mountain
Walt Disney Productions/Buena   1975
VHS

Tony and Tia are two children who can't remember where they are from. But they're clearly not from "around here," as they have telepathic powers that evil crooks want to use for dastardly ends. Luckily, they are protected by a kindly widower, who helps them find their way home. The magical children return in a sequel *Return from Witch Mountain* (in which Tony is brainwashed by a mad scientist), and a TV series.

Star rating: ❂❂

E.T. The Extra Terrestrial
PG
Universal Studios   1982
DVD; VHS

"Phone home . . ." An alien is accidentally cast away on Earth, where he is befriended by Earth-boy Elliott. Calling him E.T., Elliott teaches him Earth ways, and tries to protect him from the government scientists who are on his trail. A wonderful film that still tugs at the heartstrings today — but more adventurous viewers may prefer to ◗ to the Halloween trip and the bicycle chase. The DVD version has been fully remastered, and looks as good as new.

 Star rating: ❂❂❂❂❂

Ewok Adventure: Caravan of Courage
Lucasfilm 1984
VHS

The Towani family crash-land on the moon of Endor, and children Mace and Cindel must rescue their parents, who have been captured by the evil Gorax. Their only allies are the cuddly Ewok creatures who live there, too, but first Cindel has to convince Mace that they are friendly. A pointless, lackluster made-for-TV follow-up to **STAR WARS: EPISODE VI — RETURN OF THE JEDI**, but lacking everything except the cutesy Ewoks, which nobody liked anyway. Likely to disappoint all but the most undemanding *Star Wars* fan.

Star rating: ✪✪

Ewoks (2): Battle for Endor
Lucasfilm 1985
VHS

Cindel's entire family is killed by King Terak's army of Marauders, but she escapes with Wicket the Ewok. The pair join forces with Noa, an old man who crashed on Endor a long time ago, and they

****
★ **Credit watching:** A "Storyboard" is a ★
★ comic-book version of the film that shows ★
★ how each shot should look, to give the ★
★ filmmakers an idea before they start. ★
★ Sometimes they are only used to plan the ★
★ most complicated scenes. ★
****

prepare to fight back. Slightly more entertaining than its predecessor.

Star rating: ✪✪✪

Fairytale . . . A True Story
PG
Paramount Pictures Corp.   **1997**
VHS

Frances Griffith is sent to stay with her cousin Elsie's family during World War I. In the woods, the girls take photographs of fairies, but nobody believes that they are real. A reporter tries to find out if the girls are faking it, but discovers more than he bargained for. A sweet film for younger viewers, and supposedly based on a true story. But some viewers might find it a little slow.

Star rating: ✪✪✪

Fantasia
Walt Disney Productions/Buena   **1940**
DVD; VHS

A compilation of eight short musical pieces, preceded by a patronizing lecture about music's ability to paint pictures and tell stories. The stories it tells includes the changing seasons in the woods (Tchaikovsky), the creation of the world (Stravinsky), a village struck by evil (Mussorgsky) and people going to church (Schubert). Disney was proudest of the dancing centaurs (Beethoven). ⏩ to the "Sorcerer's Apprentice," featuring Mickey Mouse in his most famous performance, as a wizard whose attempt to clean up in record time goes seriously wrong. The voice of Mickey is provided by Walt Disney himself, who also provides a commentary from beyond the grave, with edited quotes throughout the DVD version.

 Star rating: ✪✪✪✪

Fantasia/2000

**Buena Vista Pictures Distribution, Inc.   1999
DVD; VHS**

Sixty years after the original *Fantasia*, this sequel keeps only the "Sorcerer's Apprentice" sequence, but adds many new ones. Donald Duck takes on the role of Noah (with music by Elgar), while there's an animated look at New York (Gershwin) and a beautiful pod of flying whales (Respighi), a computer-animated Hans Christian Andersen tale (Shostakovich), and a flamingo who refuses to follow the flock (Saint-Saëns). More of the same if you liked **FANTASIA**. Tons of extras on the DVD, including everything you could possibly want to know about the making of the film, bonus short cartoons, and commentaries for the grown-ups.

Star rating: ✪✪✪✪

55

Far from Home: The Adventures of Yellow Dog

PG

Twentieth Century Fox Film Corp.   1994

VHS

Canadian boy Angus adopts a stray golden retriever and calls him Yellow. While out in their boat, they are washed overboard and find themselves in uncharted forest. They begin a long trek home, surviving on bugs and beetles, but are separated before they can both get home. A heartwarming tale of a boy and his dog. Scare your parents by asking for bugs for dinner (though the filmmakers did point out at the time they only used fake ones). ⏩ to the end after Angus returns home.

Star rating: ✪✪✪

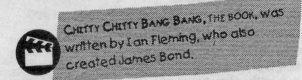

CHITTY CHITTY BANG BANG, THE BOOK, was written by Ian Fleming, who also created James Bond.

Ferngully: The Last Rainforest

Twentieth Century Fox Film Corp.   1992

DVD; VHS

Woodland creatures in an enchanted rain forest are threatened by human loggers, who have been possessed by Hexxus, the spirit of evil. But Crysta the elf befriends human boy Zak and shrinks him down to her size, in the hope that he can help her save her precious home. An obsessively green movie. Entertain adults by speculating how many rain forests were chopped down to make the film,

the video, and the packaging that came with it.
 to the song "If I'm Gonna Eat Somebody, It
Might As Well Be You." The later *Ferngully II: The
Magical Rescue*, wasn't quite up to the same
standard.

Star rating: ✪✪✪

Final Fantasy — The Spirits Within
PG-13
Columbia Pictures   2001
DVD; VHS

Earth has been attacked by alien ghosts, but Dr.
Aki Ross believes she can restore the balance by
collecting several important artifacts. But time is
running out for her — she has been infected by the
aliens and could lose her soul. Famous on release
for its lifelike computer graphics, but likely to look
old very fast as computer power constantly
improves. The fanged ghosts, with their habit of
tearing out people's souls, are likely to scare
younger viewers, but older boys will love the
chases and gunplay. to the moment the ghosts
attack Manhattan. An incredible amount of extras
on the DVD, including the cast appearing in their
own "Thriller" video. A TV series, *Final Fantasy
Unlimited*, soon followed.

Star rating: ✪✪✪

Flight of the Navigator
PG
Buena Vista Pictures Distribution, Inc.   1986
VHS

Twelve-year-old David goes looking for his brother,
Jeff, but falls down and knocks himself out. When

he comes out of the woods, eight years have passed, his family has moved, and everybody thinks he's dead. But when he starts talking to computers and regurgitating star maps, it looks as if he might have been somewhere much, much farther away. Difficult to find on video now, but a hit with pre-*X-Files* alien abductee fans.

Star rating: ✪✪

The Flintstones
PG
Universal City Studios, Inc.   1994
DVD; VHS
Stone Age construction worker Fred Flintstone is promoted at his quarry, as part of the evil Vandercave's plan to embezzle money. He falls out with his lifelong friend, Barney Rubble, and is even deserted by his wife, Wilma. Can he save the day? As with the cartoon series, *The Flintstones* relies on the idea of a normal, modern family living in a world surrounded by Stone Age jokes — such as machines made out of dinosaurs. Incredible to see the cartoon come to life, but why not just watch the cartoon again? Lots of extras on the DVD, including artwork and a "Making of" documentary.

Star rating: ✪✪

The Flintstones in Viva Rock Vegas
PG
Universal City Studios, Inc.   2000
VHS
A flashback to the time before Fred and Wilma were married. Fred and Barney have just graduated and meet up with waitress Betty and her friend Wilma (a

runaway rich girl). They go to the famous casino of Rock Vegas, but Wilma's ex-boyfriend Chip Rockefeller is intent on winning her back. Luckily, the boys have Gazoo, an alien anthropologist, to help them. A big change-around in the cast (the actors might be younger, but they were also cheaper), and, like most sequels, not as good as the original. And how does Dino get to a wedding in Rock Vegas when he wasn't on the plane?

Star rating: ✪✪

Flipper
PG
Universal City Studios, Inc.   1996
VHS

Fouteen-year-old Sandy Ricks is sent to stay with his uncle Porter, a fisherman. He rescues an orphan dolphin whose family has been killed by rival fisherman Dirk Moran, but is forced by the sheriff to let Flipper go. However, the dolphin returns feeling ill, and Sandy suspects that Dirk is dumping toxic waste out to sea. A remake of the film of the TV series, rushed out after the success of **Free Willy**. Watch for the scene where Sandy is waiting for Flipper at the docks — his Gameboy keeps magically disappearing and reappearing.

Star rating: ✪✪

Flubber
PG
Buena Vista Pictures Distribution, Inc.   1997
DVD; VHS

Professor Brainard (Robin Williams) forgets his wedding day when he stumbles across the

formula for flying rubber (flubber). But flubber
is popular stuff, and everybody wants it for
themselves, including jealous fellow scientist
Wilson, evil industrialist Hoenicker, and his two
flunkies. ⏩ to the moment when the flubber
re-creates a number of famous dance sequences.
This is a remake of a 1960 Disney film called *The
Absent-Minded Professor*. The DVD actually
re-creates the experience of the 1960s by having
nothing extra on it! **Note:** There are two occasions
where Flubber rips someone's trousers, and in
both cases, they seem magically repaired by
the next shot.

Star rating: ✪✪✪

Fly Away Home
PG
Columbia Pictures   1996
DVD; VHS

New Zealand teenager Amy loses her mother in a
car crash and must live with her estranged father
in Canada. She adopts orphan goslings in the
marshes and decides to save them, teaching
them how to migrate by leading them in a
microlight plane. This could easily have been a
sappy movie, but is actually good enough to keep

Flight Night:
DUMBO
PAULIE
PETER PAN
FLY AWAY HOME

THEME
NIGHT

the whole family watching, with some beautiful
scenery and flight sequences.

 Star rating: ✪✪✪

The Fox and the Hound
Walt Disney Productions/Buena   1981
DVD; VHS

Tod, an orphan fox cub, is adopted by the lonely
widow Tweed and befriends Copper, a hound
puppy. But their carefree childhood comes to a
sudden end when Copper begins to learn the job
he was born for . . . hunting foxes. A heartrending
Disney tale of friendship under threat, with a sad
ending close to the top of the **BAMBI** scale. The
DVD has a "Let's Be Friends" interactive read-
along and trivia game.

  Star rating: ✪✪✪

Freaky Friday
Walt Disney Productions/Buena   1976
VHS

A mother and daughter accidentally swap brains
for the day. Young Annabel finds herself in her
mother's body, while mom has to cope with her
daughter's life. **Don't ⏩** — the opening song "I'd
Like to Be You for a Day" is a winner! Good,
thought-provoking fun for parents *and* kids — just
how difficult can it be to cook dinner and go to a
business function? The original Jodie Foster version
was remade in 1995 for TV, with Gaby Hoffman as
the daughter.

 Star rating: ✪✪✪

Freddie as F.R.O.7

PG

Miramax Films   1992

VHS

A handsome prince is transformed into a frog by his wicked aunt, but this doesn't stop him from getting a job with the British secret service. With 007 off on foreign business, it is the French Freddie FRO7 who must save the day, as El Supremo the Snake Queen starts stealing monuments all over London. This British movie has the surprising ability to really annoy parents, but it might also prove to be too much for you . . . not very good.

Star rating: ✪

Free Willy

PG

Warner Bros.   1993

DVD; VHS

Cleaning up in a sea-world amusement park, reformed vandal Jesse meets Willy, a huge orca "killer whale." He soon discovers that the park owner intends to destroy Willy's tank for the insurance money — an act that will kill Willy unless Jesse can help him get to safety. Watch out for Jesse's remarkable ability to suddenly get completely dry moments after falling in the water — it happens twice! Also followed by a laughable TV cartoon series, in which Jesse and Willy fight The Machine, a cyborg intent on polluting the oceans.

Star rating: ✪✪

Free Willy 2: The Adventure Home
PG
Warner Bros.   1995
VHS

While staying up at a remote whale-tracking station, Jesse meets his human half-brother Elvis and his whale friend Willy. But Willy (and sister-whale Luna) are threatened by the oil slick from a wrecked tanker, while Elvis discovers the tanker's owners plan to capture the whales and place them back in captivity. A little more action than **FREE WILLY**, so if you wanted more of the same, here it is.

Star rating: ✪✪

Free Willy 3: The Rescue
PG
Warner Bros.   1997
VHS

Now 17, Jesse finds Willy wounded by a whaler's harpoon, but is unable to prove to the authorities that the local orcas are in danger. Luckily, he has made a friend in the form of whaler's son Max, who deliberately thwarts his own father's hunting trip. An interesting villain, because he's not the super-bad guys of the previous **FREE WILLY** movies.

But the fact this hasn't made it to DVD when the original film has ought to be something of a hint.

Star rating: ✪✪

Frog Dreaming
PG
PRD   1986
VHS

Ten-year-old Cody (played by Henry Thomas — Elliott from **E.T. THE EXTRATERRESTRIAL**) is convinced that something is alive at the bottom of a remote Australian flooded quarry called Donkegin's Hole. He believes it may have even scared an old hermit to death, while local aboriginal lore claims that the "Donkegin" is too dangerous to investigate. The film's also known as *The Quest* and is an extremely creepy movie, whatever you want to call it.

Star rating: ✪✪✪

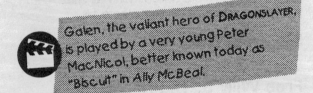

Galen, the valiant hero of DRAGONSLAYER, is played by a very young Peter MacNicol, better known today as "Biscuit" in *Ally McBeal.*

George of the Jungle
PG
Buena Vista Pictures Distribution, Inc.   1997
DVD; VHS

Rich heiress Ursula sets off into the jungle in search of the legendary "white ape." She is rescued from a lion by George, who was raised by gorillas after an air crash killed his parents. When George is wounded, Ursula takes him back to New York, where his jungle ways don't quite fit in. A fun film based on the Tarzan-like cartoon of yesteryear. Watch for Ape, a talking gorilla, and Shep, a massive elephant that thinks he's a dog. Annoy your parents by asking them how come there's an orangutan (only found in Asia) in the *African* jungle. Listen, too, for the Narrator, who gets increasingly annoyed at George's antics. Despite all the visual trickery and the chance to talk about the original 1960s cartoon series, nothing of consequence on the DVD, not even a "Making of."

 Star rating: ✪✪✪

GoBots: Battle of the Rock Lords
Atlantic Releasing Corp.   1986
VHS

Cy-Kill, a GoBot gone bad, has traveled through hyperspace to the Planet Quartex and joined forces with the evil Magmar. The rocks themselves come to life and prepare to invade Earth, but luckily Leader One and the GoBots are here to stop them. A pointless rip-off of **TRANSFORMERS**, designed to advertise toys that you can't buy anymore in stores (there was a TV series, too, before you were born). So probably best avoided. For robot fans only.

Star rating: ✪

The Golden Seal
PG
Samuel Goldwyn Company   1983
VHS

Evil hunters are determined to find a legendary golden-pelted seal in Alaska's remote Aleutian islands. Luckily, the seal has a ten-year-old boy to protect her, though the leader of the hunters is the boy's own father . . . but you might prefer to (▶) through the climactic gunfight. **FREE WILLY** meets **ANDRE**, but would you really want to watch?

Star rating: ✪✪

The Golden Voyage of Sinbad
Columbia Pictures Industries   1973
DVD; VHS

Sinbad the sailor embarks on a quest to unite the three pieces of a magical talisman before the evil sorcerer Prince Koura can use the spell to seize the throne of Marabia for himself. (▶) to the animated special effects, including a fight with a six-armed statue, and a climactic battle between a centaur and a gryphon. The extras include several mini-interviews with animator Ray Harryhausen, more likely to interest the grown-ups. See also the **SEVENTH VOYAGE OF SINBAD**.

Star rating: ✪✪✪

The Goonies
PG
Warner Bros.   1995
DVD; VHS

When land developers prepare to demolish their homes, seven kids stumble across a map to find buried treasure. But they have to get to it before the notorious Fratelli crime family. A real roller-coaster ride (complete with people screaming a lot). Watch for the scene in the restaurant, where Mikey says to

Brand, "There is something buried under there, Josh." (He accidentally used actor Josh Brolin's real name). Keep an eye on Sloth's teeth, too. They change throughout the movie. The DVD is loaded with extras, including a "Making of," a pop video, a commentary, and deleted scenes (including the octopus mentioned in the film, but not seen in the original release).

 Star rating: ✪✪✪✪

Gordy
Miramax Films   1994
VHS

Gordy the talking pig must try to rescue his parents from the slaughterhouse. En route he is adopted by a human family and becomes known as the Hero Pig when he saves one of their lives. Often panned for ripping off **Babe**, this film was actually released before the more famous pig movie. Stay away from the climactic scene in the slaughterhouse — it could turn you and all your friends into vegetarians.

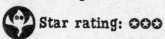 **Star rating: ✪✪✪**

The Great Muppet Caper
Afd/Universal City Studios, Inc.   1981
DVD; VHS

"Miss Piggy, you're overacting! You're hamming it up!" Kermit the Frog, Fozzie Bear, and Gonzo the Magnificent are three reporters on the trail of a jewel thief, while Nicky Holiday (Charles Grodin, yes, the dad from **Beethoven**) has fallen head-over-heels in love with Miss Piggy. More great laughs, singable songs, and excruciating puns for all the family. The DVD, however, has even less than the first, just a few Muppetisms again, and those with good audio systems will be disappointed to know that all the speakers only come alive during the musical numbers. Annoy your parents by asking how a bear and a frog can be "identical twins."

  Star rating: ✪✪✪

Harriet the Spy
PG
Paramount Pictures Corp.   1996
VHS

Obsessive note-taker Harriet is accused by her classmates of being a spy. She gets her revenge on them, but her former nanny Ole Golly explains that sometimes people don't want to hear the truth about themselves. A film that can drag a little — ▶ to the revenge thing, which takes a whole hour to arrive. Befuddle your parents by asking how Harriet can have her diary returned to her when you've already seen her destroying it in her room.

Star rating: ✪✪

★★★★★★★★★★★★★★★★★★★★★★★★★★★★★★★★
★ **Credit watching:** The "Boom Operator" is ★
★ the person who holds the "boom mike," a ★
★ microphone on the end of a long pole that ★
★ is held above the actors' heads. ★
★★★★★★★★★★★★★★★★★★★★★★★★★★★★★★★★

Harry and the Hendersons
PG
Universal City Studios, Inc.   1987
VHS

The Henderson family is on vacation when their car collides with a real-life Bigfoot. Nursing him back to life in their Seattle home, they find that he is a gentle giant, though one prone to wreck their entire house, and extremely popular with local hunters and nosy neighbors. Later followed by a disappointing TV series.

 Star rating: ✪✪

Harry Potter and the Sorcerer's Stone
PG
Warners Bros.   2001
DVD; VHS

Harry Potter discovers he is really a wizard and is packed off to the elite Hogwarts School, in a long film that does its level best to re-create the book — making it more of an exercise in comparison than a movie experience. You'll find yourself pleased with the depiction of Hagrid the giant, disappointed there isn't more of the magical sport Quidditch, and wondering after a couple of hours how much of the book you could have actually sat down and read in that time. Watch for the bishop's strange behavior in the chess game — I thought they were supposed to move *diagonally*.

 Star rating: ✪✪✪

Heidi's Song
Paramount Pictures Corp.   1982
VHS

Heidi goes to live with her grandfather in the mountains, but her happiness is disrupted when she is sent away to the city. The story of *Heidi* has been filmed more than a dozen times, and adults will insist that the TV series or the Shirley Temple black-and-white movie is the best. This animated version's not the easiest to find, though, but better than the so-called *New Adventures of Heidi*, which takes place in New York! ❿ to the nightmare sequence — the best bit in an otherwise dull film.

Star rating: ✪✪

Help, I'm a Fish
Film aPs/Egmont et al.   2000
VHS

Fly's sister Stella accidentally drinks a potion, invented by Professor MacKrill, to help humans breath underwater. She turns into a starfish and is thrown into the sea, and Fly must drink the potion and chase after her — but he only has 48 hours, or he will stay a fish forever. ❿ to the point where evil pilot-fish Joe seizes control of an undersea city in a sunken liner, causing a massive synchronized swimming event right out of the old-time musicals. If you want to see this one, you'll need to find it on TV — it's not available on video in the United States yet.

Star rating: ⊙⊙

Hercules
Buena Vista Pictures Distribution, Inc.   1997
DVD; VHS

The mortal Hercules must become a hero if he is ever to become a god. He becomes flavor of the moment when he defeats the many-headed Hydra, but when he falls for the pretty Meg, she turns out to be a damsel in a lot more distress than he first thought. Hades, the god of the underworld, is holding her soul to ransom. Look for the lion's pelt Hercules wears (it looks suspiciously like the evil Scar from THE LION KING), and hidden Mickey Mouse seekers should stand on their heads and watch the hairdo of one of the chorus girls. The lack of extras on the DVD is a Greek tragedy, though viewers do get a "Making of" featurette.

 Star rating: ⊙⊙⊙

The Hobbit
Warner Bros   1977
DVD

Bilbo Baggins is recruited as a burglar by Gandalf the wizard, who wants him to help a group of dwarfs steal treasure from Smaug, the dragon who rules Lonely Mountain. This little-known cartoon was rushed out onto DVD after the success of the LORD OF THE RINGS: FELLOWSHIP OF THE RING movie in 2001, but it's nowhere near the same league. Fun for the younger viewers, but beware of the painful songs.

 Star rating: ✪✪

Home Alone
PG
Twentieth Century Fox Film Corp.   **1990**
DVD; VHS

The last thing that Kevin wants to do is go on the family vacation to Paris. He gets his wish when his parents forget to take him and he is left home alone, while two burglars try to break in. Luckily, he has a whole arsenal of very painful, very dangerous, and very funny tricks up his sleeve to keep them out. Reassure your parents by promising you won't be trying *any* of this at home — alone or otherwise, and ask yourself how Kevin can dial out for pizza when the phone lines are down. DVD "extras" are trailers for the other **HOME ALONE** films . . . well, whoopee.

Star rating: ✪✪

Home Alone 2: Lost in New York
PG
Twentieth Century Fox Film Corp.   **1992**
DVD; VHS

Well, there's a surprise. Kevin is split from his neglectful parents *again*. While they fly to Florida, he finds himself in New York. And by an *amazing* coincidence, the same two burglars from the last film are trying to break into a toy store. More pain, and more guilty laughs at adults' expense, but you're smart enough to know that this is just an attempt to get more money out of you, right? Impress adults by noticing there's already a mark

72

on Marv's forehead before a thrown brick even hits him, and astound them by explaining that the mark came from a brick that was thrown earlier, but then cut.

Star rating: ✪

Alan Parker's children complained he wouldn't take them to see *The Godfather*, so he rewrote it with a young cast and no blood – the result was BUGSY MALONE.

Home Alone 3
PG

Twentieth Century Fox Film Corp.   1997
DVD; VHS

Different boy, different crooks, but same old same-old. Young Alex gets chicken pox and is left at home by his working parents. Watch for the moment when he runs outside (seemingly magically changing from pajamas into coat and gloves, then back again when he comes indoors). The filmmakers don't seem to have been that bothered by the mistake or by the fact that this is just a higher-tech rip-off of the earlier films. More violent "humor" that at times is painful to watch.

Star rating: ✪

Homeward Bound:
The Incredible Journey
Buena Vista Pictures Distribution, Inc.   1992
VHS

Chance the puppy, Shadow the older dog, and Sassy the prissy cat are accidentally abandoned by their owners. They decide to head off to San Francisco to find them. Some pretty dangerous don't-try-this-at-home moments — including Sassy going over a waterfall and Chance's unpleasant encounter with a porcupine. Listen out for **BACK TO THE FUTURE**'s Michael J. Fox as the voice of Chance.

Star rating: ✪✪✪

Honey, I Shrunk the Kids
PG
Buena Vista Pictures Distribution, Inc.   1989
VHS

Absentminded Professor Wayne Szalinski doesn't realize that his own kids have been shrunk by his latest invention. After he throws them in the garbage, they must cross the yard. But that's not as easy as it sounds, since they have to contend with giant bees, a massive flood from a garden hose, and other threats that will scare younger viewers but will let older ones have a whale of a time. Watch when the kids are riding on the bug — you can actually see people moving it from off-screen.

 Star rating: ✪✪✪✪

Honey, I Blew Up the Kid
PG
Buena Vista Pictures Distribution, Inc.   1992
VHS

No points for guessing that the Professor's latest invention actually makes things bigger than they ought to be. Cue the attack of the 112-foot baby, but this is nowhere near as good as **HONEY, I SHRUNK THE KIDS**.

Star rating: ✪

Honey, We Shrunk Ourselves

PG

Buena Vista Home Video   1996

VHS

This time, the kids stay normal size while their parents shrink down to keep a secret eye on them. Because it's more dangerous for them, it's more fun for you — cue attacking cockroaches, flying soap bubbles, and a scary ride in a toy car. Still not as good as the first film, but even though made straight-to-video, a vast improvement on **HONEY, I BLEW UP THE KID.** Watch for the hand poking out of the "hot-dog volcano" — another case of "hidden help" for special effects. **(▶)** to the toy car — Hot Wheels toys will never seem the same again!

Star rating: ✪✪

Hook

PG

TriStar Pictures   1991

DVD; VHS

Many years after the events of **PETER PAN**, Peter has grown up! He is married to Wendy's grand-daughter and has kids of his own. But he must return to Never Land when one of them is kidnapped by his old enemy Captain Hook. It sounds good . . . but it does *seem* to go on forever. Watch for the moment when Hook slashes Peter's arm — watch it in slow-mo to see the "metal" hook behaving very strangely. **(▶)** to the massive battle on Hook's pirate ship. The DVD includes a "Making of" and a Lost Treasure game.

Star rating: ✪✪

The Hunchback of Notre Dame
Buena Vista Pictures Distribution, Inc.   1996
VHS

Hunchback bell ringer Quasimodo has lived in Notre Dame cathedral since his gypsy mother was killed by Frollo, evil Chief of Justice in Paris. Frollo's right-hand man, Captain of the Guard Phoebus, falls in love with the gypsy girl Esmerelda, and Quasimodo helps them both when Frollo plans a secret attack on the city's gypsy quarter. As with many Disney films, the hero has some excellent, comic friends — in this case three talking gargoyles who keep him company. And watch for cameos from other cartoons, especially during the song "Out There" — Belle from **BEAUTY AND THE BEAST**, the Carpet from **ALADDIN**, and Pumbaa from **THE LION KING**. Watch for hidden Mickey Mouses in a bunch of grapes and on a pillar. A video sequel features Quasimodo falling in love with a beautiful girl who is forced to steal a bell from his cathedral.

 Star rating: ✪✪✪

The Indian in the Cupboard
PG
Paramount Pictures Corp.   1995
DVD; VHS

Nine-year-old boy Omri is given the key to a magic cupboard that brings his model American Indian (Little Bear) to life. But when his friend Patrick demands a living figure of his own (a cowboy called Boone), there's trouble in the toy box. A mixture of the little-people adventure in **TOY STORY** and the Indian morals of **POCAHONTAS**. Surprisingly good fun. Director Frank Oz provides a commentary for the DVD (more for the grown-ups, though you may recognize the voice — he is better known for playing Fozzie Bear and Yoda).

 Star rating: ✪✪✪✪

Indiana Jones and the Raiders of the Lost Ark

PG

Paramount Pictures Corp.   1981

VHS

Hitler sends Nazi agents to recover the Ark of the Covenant, an artifact said to make an army invincible. Only American archaeologist Indiana Jones (played by Harrison Ford) can stop them, in a globe-trotting adventure that takes him from Nepal to Egypt, with time out in the sweltering jungles of South America. One of the best adventure movies ever made, with plenty to entertain you, the parents, the grandparents, and even great-grandparents. Action-packed, with gunfights, chases, punch-outs, a liberal dose of creepy-crawlies, just enough kissing stuff to keep the romantics happy, and some terrifying shocks that will have the youngsters hiding behind the sofa. Originally known as *Raiders of the Lost Ark*, but renamed to fit in with the rest of the series.

  Star rating: ✪✪✪✪✪

Indiana Jones and the Temple of Doom

PG-13

Paramount Pictures Corp.   1984

VHS

Rather disappointing prequel to the original, with Indiana Jones on the run from Chinese gangsters, volunteering to save an Indian village from the evil cult leader Mola Ram. Where the first film was scary in places, this one takes things a little too far for younger family members and is best avoided by the fainthearted. Watch out for the club where Willie performs her stunning opening number — it's called Club Obi-Wan, in a reference to producer George Lucas's **STAR WARS**. Annoy parents by pointing out that Indiana Jones doesn't believe in magic in **INDIANA JONES AND THE RAIDERS OF THE LOST ARK**, even though that film is supposed to take place *after* the magical ending of this one.

 Star rating: ✪✪✪

Indiana Jones and the Last Crusade

PG-13

Paramount Pictures Corp.   1989

VHS

This is the *real* sequel to **INDIANA JONES AND THE RAIDERS OF THE LOST ARK**! Nazi treasure hunters are looking for the Holy Grail and kidnap the world Grail expert, Indiana's Dad Henry Jones. To rescue him and save the world, Indiana must journey to the heart of Nazi Germany and out into the Turkish

★★★★★★★★★★★★★★★★★★★★★★★★★★★★★★★★
★ **Credit watching:** A "Continuity" person is ★
★ in charge of making sure that everything ★
★ matches from scene-to-scene, that ★
★ actors are in the right places, costumes ★
★ and hairstyles don't change, or that ★
★ background items haven't moved. ★
★★★★★★★★★★★★★★★★★★★★★★★★★★★★★★★★

wilderness. Almost as much fun as the original film. (After the events here, Harrison Ford briefly appeared once more in the TV movie *Indiana Jones and the Mystery of the Blues* — part of the excellent *Young Indiana Jones* TV series.)

  Star rating: ✪✪✪

Inspector Gadget
PG
Buena Vista Pictures Distribution, Inc.   1999
DVD; VHS

Security guard John Brown is almost killed when the evil Scolex steals Professor Bradford's invention. Bradford's daughter Brenda saves John's life by giving him mechanical implants — he is now the crime-fighter Inspector Gadget. Scolex, however, (now called the Claw) invents Robogadget to defeat him. Plenty of fantastic inventions, battles, and gags — including some very obscure ones. Listen out for a hospital announcer paging doctors Howard, Fine, and Howard (the Three Stooges) and oodles of cameos from movie bad-guys of yesteryear. The DVD includes a "Making of" and a music video.

 Star rating: ✪✪✪

The Iron Giant
PG
Warner Bros.   1999
DVD; VHS

Nine-year-old Hogarth Hughes befriends a giant metal man who falls out of the sky and asks grown-up Dean to let him hide the giant in his junkyard. The giant means no harm, but government agent Kent Mansley refuses to believe it and orders the military to attack. When that fails, Kent prepares a nuclear attack, and only the giant can save Hogarth's entire town. Good fun for everybody who ever wanted a talking toy that could assemble itself and fight off the local army. The DVD includes a "Making of" and a music video.

 Star rating: ✪✪✪✪

James and the Giant Peach
PG
Buena Vista Pictures Distribution, Inc.   1996
DVD; VHS

Young James is adopted by evil aunts after his parents are eaten by a rhinoceros (don't laugh, it could happen to you). He escapes from them by climbing inside a giant peach, which rolls into the sea with him aboard, along with a group of friendly insects. A darkly entertaining film based on Roald Dahl's book, starting off in live-action before changing to animation. ⏭ to the scene on the haunted ship for Jack Skellington, the hero of the same production company's **NIGHTMARE BEFORE CHRISTMAS**, as well as a skeleton that looks suspiciously like Donald Duck! The DVD has a rather poor "Making of" and a music video as extras, but that's better than nothing.

Star rating: ✪✪✪

Jason and the Argonauts
Columbia Pictures Industries   1963
DVD; VHS

Jason, heir to the throne of Thessaly, is sent to
Colchis to find the mythical Golden Fleece. But
rival factions of gods will do anything to stop
him — including battles with flying harpies, a giant
bronze colossus, a hydra, and, the ⏵ highlight of
them all, a swordfight with skeletons. The DVD
includes an interview with Ray Harryhausen, the
master craftsman who made and animated the
monsters.

   Star rating: ✪✪✪✪

The Journey of Natty Gann
PG
Buena Vista Distribution Co.   1985
VHS

Tough young Chicago girl Natty is left behind when
her father heads off to find work in 1930s Seattle.
She escapes from her unpleasant guardian and
falls in with a group of thieves while riding the
railroad. Captured and sent to an orphanage, she
must escape again and set off in search of her
father, accompanied by her newest friend . . . a
huge wolf. Cussing, fighting, and harrowing
moments all combine to make this a Disney best
kept away from the youngest viewers. No longer
on sale on video, so only likely to be found
secondhand, rental, or on TV.

Star rating: ✪✪

Archer, the computer-generated alien in SMALL SOLDIERS, required 62 times the computing power that animated the Tyrannosaurus Rex in JURASSIC PARK.

Jumanji

PG
TriStar Pictures   1995
DVD; VHS

Judy and Peter Shepherd are moving into their new house when they find the Victorian board game Jumanji. When they start to play it, they release Alan, a boy who has been trapped inside the game for 26 years. Now they must play the game through to the end, though the hazards it presents come to life in the real world! A spectacular special-effects movie, with time out for stampeding wild animals, a typhoon, and a hunter escaping from the game to hunt the children in the real world. A little scary for the young ones. Followed by a rather less impressive TV series and the film *Jumanji 2*, out in 2002. The DVD "Collector's Edition" includes a commentary and three different "Making of" documentaries, concentrating on the fabulous special effects.

 Star rating: ✪✪✪

The Jungle Book

Walt Disney Productions/Buena   1967
DVD; VHS

Human orphan Mowgli is abandoned in the jungle and raised by wolves. Bagheera the panther decides to return him to his own kind, but realizes that Mowgli prefers it in the forest, with marching elephants, singing monkeys, and his old pal Baloo the dancing bear. to the great songs, including "I Wanna Be Like You" and the Oscar-nominated "Bear Necessities" — and keep a watchful eye on the adults, because the chances are high they'll start singing along. There have also been two live-action versions, starring Sabu and Jason Scott Lee as Mowgli. The DVD edition contains no extras worth speaking of.

  Star rating: ✪✪✪✪

Jurassic Park
PG-13
Universal City Studios, Inc.   1993
DVD; VHS

Dinosaurs are brought back to life by a theme-park owner, but run amok when human greed sets them free. through the first half hour — *yeah, yeah*, "DNA sequencing," *blah blah*, "welcome to the park . . ." You don't want the science part, you want a *Tyrannosaurus rex* demolishing a toilet and raptors chasing the park owner's grandchildren through a kitchen. As one might expect from the director of the **INDIANA JONES** movies, the action never stops, but dinosaurs are scary creatures, and this very realistic film was deemed too scary for the director's *own* children. The DVD is absolutely packed with extras, including a "Making of," test animations, storyboards, and artwork.

 Star rating: ✪✪✪✪

THEME NIGHT

Dino Night:
JURASSIC PARK
DINOSAUR
THE LAND BEFORE TIME
JURASSIC PARK 2: THE LOST WORLD

Jurassic Park 2: The Lost World
PG-13
Universal City Studios, Inc.   1997
DVD; VHS

Near Isla Nubar (the original **JURASSIC PARK**), is Isla Sorna, the secret test facility. Mathematician Ian Malcolm, a survivor from the original team, goes there to help document the dinosaurs, but an eco-warrior sets some free. Some handy lessons ensue about not stealing baby T. rexes (you knew not to do that, right?). More fun for those who like watching dinosaurs eat people, but not as good as the original. The DVD includes a "Making of," storyboards, and a "Dinosaur Encyclopaedia."

 Star rating: ✪✪

Jurassic Park III
PG-13
Universal City Studios, Inc.   2001
DVD; VHS

Isla Sorna isn't so secret anymore, and young Eric Kirby crashes there after a paragliding accident. His rich father organizes a mission to retrieve him, which includes original team member (yes, another one) Alan Grant. Then they arrive and things go wrong, and . . . look, the filmmakers spent a lot of money on the dinosaurs, so they want to use them a few times. If you want to see more dinosaurs eating people, and a definite do-not-try-this-at-home trick with a mobile phone, this is your chance. But why not just watch the original three times? Confuse adults by pointing out that, with the pterodactyls caged on the island at the beginning, (a) they couldn't have attacked the boat, and (b) they would have starved to death years earlier.

 Star rating: ✪✪

Kiki's Delivery Service
Buena Vista Home Entertainment   1998 VHS

Thirteen-year-old Kiki must live for a year in a strange town to prove that she has what it takes to be a witch. Accompanied by her cat, Jiji, she starts up a flying-broomstick courier service, much to the surprise of the local inhabitants. A simply wonderful cartoon — beautifully made and charming to the last, though audience members will wait in vain for giant robots or alien invaders.

 Star rating: ✪✪✪✪✪

★★★★★★★★★★★★★★★★★★★★★★★★★★★★★★★
★ **Credit watching:** A "Pyrotechnician" is in ★
★ charge of bangs. That includes big ones ★
★ like exploding buildings, all the way down ★
★ to little "squibs" (the things that make it ★
★ look like someone has been shot by a ★
★ bullet). ★
★★★★★★★★★★★★★★★★★★★★★★★★★★★★★★★

The King and I
Warner Bros.   1999
VHS

British widow Anna becomes a tutor to the children of the King of Siam. But she is soon swept up in palace intrigues, as the Crown Prince falls in love with a servant girl and the King's aide "the Kralahome" makes a bid for the throne. A poor animated attempt to imitate the famous musical, complete with a few halfhearted funny animals, and (for those who've seen the original) a major character who is still alive at the end. ⏩ to the famous songs, such as "Shall We Dance?" which are still intact. If it's so bad, why is it here? Because adults will tell you that you should watch this cartoon version, but frankly, you'd be better off with the Yul Brynner live-action one *they* think is too old for you. Other versions of the same story include *Anna and the King*, starring Chow Yun-Fat as the king, and *Anna and the King of Siam*, starring Rex Harrison.

 Star rating: ✪

Krull
PG
Columbia Pictures Industries   1983
DVD; VHS

Prince Colwyn must gather a band of adventurers to save Princess Lyssa from the Beast, a fiendishly ugly creature that has sent his Slayers to kidnap her and then imprisoned her in his flying fortress. A great swashbuckling fantasy adventure, complete with giant spiders, a cyclops, and some spectacular laser battles. Look out for Liam Neeson (Qui-Gon Jinn from STAR WARS: EPISODE I — THE PHANTOM MENACE) hanging around in a small role. The DVD contains lots of commentaries and a "Making of."

Star rating: ✪✪✪

Labyrinth
PG
TriStar Pictures   1986
DVD; VHS

Sarah must cross a fearsome maze to save her brother Toby from Jareth, the evil Goblin King, in a film that mixes human actors and muppets from Jim Henson's studio. ⏩ to the best song "Dance Magic Dance," in which David Bowie really struts his stuff as the Goblin King. Look out for the pop-star posters on the wall in Sarah's bedroom — is that David Bowie we can see!? Also watch for the moment when Sarah escapes from the dungeon, and Jareth throws off his disguise — he throws it off twice. The DVD contains a fabulous "Making of" documentary.

 Star rating: ✪✪✪

Lady and the Tramp
Walt Disney Productions/Buena   1955
DVD; VHS

Lady, the well-bred cocker spaniel, is displaced by a new arrival in her home (a *human* baby, urgh!) and blamed when the evil Siamese cats wreck the living room. She runs away and falls in with tough street-mongrel Tramp. On her way home after a magical evening, she is thrown in the dog pound, and her adventures are only just beginning. No fast-forwarding here, though you might like to memorize

Escape from the KIDS section #2: Westerns
Would you rather saddle up and ride out of the
one-horse kiddie town? Then you'd better start
with *Shane*, *The Searchers*, *High Noon*, and
The Magnificent Seven. For a more modern
look at the same material, try *Silverado*.

where to find the song "We Are Siamese If You
Please" for your own enjoyment.

  Star rating: ✪✪✪✪✪

Lady and the Tramp II: Scamp's Adventure

Buena Vista Home Entertainment   2000
DVD; VHS

Lady and the Tramp have four puppies — three
girls, who look like their mother, and Scamp, a
boy who looks like his dad. Scamp is a rebel who
would rather be a junkyard dog, but eventually
he sees the error of his ways. The DVD includes a
commentary, a "Making of," an interactive game,
and three Disney shorts starring Mickey Mouse's
dog Pluto — not bad.

 Star rating: ✪✪✪

Ladyhawke

PG-13
Warner Bros.   1984
VHS

Pickpocket Phillipe "The Mouse" Gaston is the
unlikely new traveling companion of Navarre, a
knight cursed never to see his ladylove Isabeau

again — he becomes a wolf each night, and she becomes a hawk each day, while both are pursued by the evil bishop. A love story with plenty of sword-fights — who could ask for more? The DVD extras are a trifle low-tech, but do include page after page of trivia and production gossip.

 Star rating: ✪✪✪✪

Knight Night:
THE PRINCESS BRIDE
WILLOW
LADYHAWKE
KRULL

The Land Before Time
Universal City Studios, Inc.   1988
DVD; VHS

Littlefoot the orphan apatosaurus has lost his family but gained a new group of friends — Cera the triceratops, Ducky the hadrosaur, Petrie the pterodactyl, and Spike the stegosaurus. Together they must travel the long distance to the fabled Great Valley.

 Star rating: ✪✪✪

The Land Before Time II: The Great Valley Adventure
Universal City Studios, Inc.   1994
DVD; VHS

All is not well in the Great Valley. Thieves have stolen a dinosaur egg, and although the young dinosaurs can retrieve it, they accidentally make it possible for two deadly Sharptooths to enter the valley. A very disappointing sequel.

 Star rating: ✪

The Land Before Time III: The Time of the Great Giving
Universal City Studios, Inc.   1995
DVD; VHS

A meteorite crashes into the land nearby (hang on . . . this is suspiciously like **DINOSAUR**) and the inhabitants of the Great Valley must cooperate — leaving the safety of the valley in order to restore their water supply. More fun than the previous sequel, thanks to some scary raptors.

 Star rating: ✪✪

The Land Before Time IV: The Journey Through the Mists
MCA Home Entertainment   1996
VHS

Dire follow-up in which Littlefoot must go on a quest to cure his grandfather's illness. The baddies aren't much fun (a crocodile! We can see one of those in **PETER PAN**!), and there is the unwelcome introduction of some apatosaurus kissing stuff. Avoid. Go straight to the next one. There's another one!? Actually, there are *three* more: *The Mysterious Island*, *The Secret of Saurus Rock*, and *The Stone of Cold Fire* — but they never get more interesting than **THE LAND BEFORE TIME III**, and that itself wasn't as good as the original movie. If you like the songs, though, a far better time can be had with *The Land Before Time Sing-Along Songs* and *More Sing-Along Songs* tapes, which are also available.

 Star rating: ✪

 Mr. Dewey, the magical librarian in THE PAGEMASTER, is named after Melvil Dewey, the inventor of the system libraries use to keep books in order.

Lassie Come Home
MGM Film Company   1943
VHS

A family of city slickers move out to the country, where son Matt befriends the collie dog Lassie. Lassie turns out to be smarter than the local humans, especially when it comes to thwarting the evil activities of a local sheep farmer. Although there's a happy ending, it comes after some harrowing scenes that may disturb the young ones (and any other dog lovers present). The 1994 remake is only slightly easier to find on video than the equally entertaining 1943 original *Lassie Come Home*. There are several TV series as well.

 Star rating: ✪✪✪

The Last Flight of Noah's Ark
Walt Disney Productions/Buena   1980
DVD; VHS

A missionary, a pilot, and a group of kids crash-land on a Pacific Island inhabited by Japanese soldiers who don't realize the Second World War is over. Once that's settled, everyone helps out to get the group back to civilization. ▶ to the encounter with a shark. Not much on the DVD (looks like the release company doesn't realize the days of sappy extras are over, too).

Star rating: ✪✪✪

The Last Starfighter
PG
Universal City Studios, Inc.   1984
DVD; VHS

Teenager Alex Rogan is obsessed with video games, but seems doomed to spend his life in his dead-end town. That's until he discovers that his gaming is a secret test for star fighters — space soldiers needed to fight a war against alien invaders. ▶ to the arrival of Alex's mentor Centauri — that's when the space battles start in earnest. Great fun, with cool extras, including a photo gallery, crew commentaries, and a 30-minute "Making of."

Star rating: ✪✪✪

The Last Unicorn
Jensen Farley Pictures, Inc.   1982
VHS

The last unicorn in the world sets off to find others of her kind (oh . . . so she's only *maybe* the Last Unicorn, then). En route she meets Schmendrick, the hapless magician, and handsome human Prince Lir, who do their best to help her resist the evil King Haggard. A surprising treat for adults and children alike.

  Star rating: ✪✪✪

The Lion King
Buena Vista Pictures Distribution, Inc.   1994
VHS

Lion Prince Simba is left for dead after his uncle Scar murders his father, King Mufasa. However, he is cared for by meerkat Timon and smelly warthog Pumbaa, who teach him the values of goofing off before he goes back to reclaim his kingdom. After a stunning opening sequence (the Oscar-nominated "Circle of Life" song), the film settles into a standard Disney-movie pattern — it's one of the better ones from the recent run of Disney cartoons. Look for hidden Mickey Mouses in the stars and treetops. Amaze adults by noting that nothing changes in *The Lion King*: hyenas are always evil, lions are always in charge, and the zebras that bow before the king are probably going to be his lunch the next day.

 Star rating: ✪✪✪✪

The Lion King 2: Simba's Pride
Walt Disney Productions   1998
DVD; VHS

Simba's daughter Kiara is forced to leave the Pride Lands and wander the Outlands. Luckily she has Timon and Pumbaa for company, and eventually overcomes the obstacles in her path and finds true love. So . . . er . . . an exact copy of the first film, then. The DVD is almost devoid of extras — *Simba's Lack of Pride*, more like.

Star rating: ✪✪

The Lion, the Witch, and the Wardrobe
DPI/Children's Television Workshop   1979
VHS

Four children cross over into the magical world of Narnia (found at the back of their wardrobe), which is held in the icy grip of the coldhearted White Witch. They join forces with Aslan the good lion, leader of the other mythical beasts, and become knights for good in an enchanted realm. Cheap animation, but the original story still shines through. No video available in the United States yet, but you may be able to find this on TV.

Star rating: ✪✪✪

The Little Mermaid
Buena Vista Pictures Distribution, Inc.   1989
DVD; VHS

Princess Ariel lives under the sea with her father, the sea-king Triton. She rescues the human prince Eric from a shipwreck. Her companion, Sebastian the crab, accidentally tells Triton that she is in love with a human, and she is forbidden from seeing Eric ever again. Ursula the witch offers to turn her into a human, but without a voice — giving her three days to get a kiss from Eric or else she will belong to Ursula for eternity. ⏵ to the bit where Ursula becomes enormous — if you fancy being really scared for five minutes! Otherwise, leave it for the little ones. Good fun and some good songs like the Oscar-nominated "Under the Sea," but also some corny ones like the Oscar-winning "Kiss the Girl." Look among the crowd scene at the concert for some special guests. Predictable levels of kissing stuff, and almost no extras on the DVD — something that could have been mer-made better.

 Star rating: ✪✪✪

The Little Mermaid 2
Buena Vista Home Entertainment   2000
DVD; VHS

Ariel's half-human daughter Melody is not allowed near the sea, but she runs away, dives back into her ancestral home, and has an underwater adventure. However, Ursula's sister, Morgana, has a secret plan of her own to seize control of the seas, and has to be stopped by the old gang, with a couple of new members. Four new songs . . . and a *slight* twist on the original plot. The DVD includes games and a storybook.

 Star rating: ✪✪

A Little Princess
Warner Bros.   1994
DVD; VHS

Rich girl Sarah Crewe, a captain's daughter, is sent to Miss Minchin's boarding school in New York. There, she wins over most of her classmates with her skills at storytelling — and the many gifts her father sends her. But when her father goes missing,

Sarah is deprived of everything and thrown out of the school, forced to rely on the kindness of her former friends and her Indian neighbor Ram Dass. An Edwardian **CINDERELLA** in reverse, but with a happy ending nonetheless. ⏩ to the moments when Sarah entertains her classmates with tales from the Ramayana — an Indian classic. The DVD includes "production notes" — hardly a royal treatment.

Star rating: ✪✪✪

The Little Vampire
New Line Cinema   2000
DVD; VHS

American Tony Thompson moves with his parents to Scotland, where he befriends local boy Rudolph, a young vampire. Hiding Rudolph from Rookery the vampire hunter, Tony discovers that a magical amulet can restore Rudolph to life if he can obtain it before the fly-past of a comet in a few days. A dark-but-fun bloodsucking tale. ⏩ to the vampire cows. Yes, cows. The DVD includes three interactive games, a compendium of ghoulish jokes, and recipes for spooky snacks.

Star rating: ✪✪✪

Little Women
PG
Columbia Pictures   1994
DVD; VHS

Frocks and tea parties abound, as the Massachusetts March family struggles on while the

Civil War rages elsewhere. Mrs. March's four daughters are very different — a prissy madame, a would-be writer, a musical prodigy, and a self-absorbed artist, but they all muddle through eventually. Impress adults by wondering aloud if Jo the writer is based on the original author of the book (she was). Adults will probably complain that the "original" film version with Elizabeth Taylor was a lot better, and it was, but only slightly. There are several other film versions and at least two cartoons, as well. Hardly anything on the DVD — *Little Thought*.

Star rating: ✪✪

The Lord of the Rings
PG
United Artists   1978
DVD

A group of humans, hobbits, and elves volunteers to escort Frodo Baggins across Middle-earth to dispose of a magical ring before it can cause the end of the world. This early adaptation of J.R.R. Tolkien's book was billed as a cartoon, but consisted largely of "rotoscoping" — drawing a cartoon over the top of a live-action film. Buyers beware: In some countries, the box merely has the logo, no pictures from the film, which could fool you into thinking you were buying the more recent version. The filmmakers ran out of money and stopped halfway (during *The Two Towers*), but this half-cartoon/half-live hybrid will still keep Middle-earth fans happy while they wait for the next live-action installment. Listen for the voice of Legolas — that's Antony Daniels (C3PO from *Star Wars*). Also for the occasions when some cast members mistakenly refer to Saruman as "Aruman." See also **THE RETURN OF THE KING**.

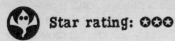 Star rating: ✪✪✪

The Lord of the Rings: The Fellowship of the Ring
PG-13
New Line Cinema   2001
DVD; VHS

Frodo Baggins discovers his precious ring is actually a powerful magical item, whose evil original owner wants it back. He goes on the run with a group of elves, dwarfs, humans, and fellow hobbits, pursued by a series of deadly foes. A film guaranteed to scare the pants off the younger ones in the audience, and quite a few of the adults, too — not recommended for young children. ⏩ through the Shire — birthday parties are less interesting than Ringwraiths, Cave Trolls, and the Giant Orcs, and you'll shave nearly an hour off! Director Peter Jackson appears twice in his own film — once as Bilbo's father in a photo on the mantelpiece, and again as Bree walking past the Prancing Pony Inn. Followed by *The Two Towers* (2002) and **THE RETURN OF THE KING** (2003).

 Star rating: ✪✪✪✪✪

The Love Bug
Walt Disney Productions/Buena   1968
VHS

Jim Douglas, a San Francisco racing driver down on his luck, discovers that his car Herbie has a mind of its own. Made in the 1960s, so be prepared for some weird haircuts and strange pants. That's no excuse for the low level of extras on the DVD, though. Sequels include *Herbie Rides Again*, *Herbie Goes to Monte Carlo*, *Herbie Goes Bananas*, and the short-lived *Love Bug* TV series. Dean Jones (Jim), turns up in the 1990s as a bad guy in **BEETHOVEN**.

Star rating: ✪✪

Mac and Me
PG
Orion Pictures Corp.
VHS   1988

Shameless rip-off of **E.T. THE EXTRA TERRESTRIAL** in which a "Mysterious Alien Creature" (MAC) is marooned in California and befriends a local boy. This film gained its first star for the sensible portrayal of a disabled child (wheelchair-bound actor Jade Calegory genuinely has spina bifida) and its second for its sneakiness. If you are unfortunate enough to watch it, see if you can count how many hidden ads there are in the film. Award yourself points every time it tries to sell you Coke or a well-known fast-food hamburger. ◗ to the song-and-dance number in McDonalds — possibly the lowest moment in cinema history.

Star rating: ✪✪

Madeline

PG

Tristar Pictures   1998

DVD; VHS

Orphan Madeline is the littlest pupil at Miss Clavel's all-girl school, who organizes the other students when their late benefactor's husband plots to sell it off. She is kidnapped when she tries to save Pepito, the Spanish ambassador's son, from crooks but manages to escape with him on a motorbike. But though she can save herself, can she save the school? A little disjointed (because it's based on four books, crushed into one another), but lots of fun. The TV cartoon series was even better. The DVD includes a much earlier 1952 cartoon version as an extra.

Star rating: ✪✪✪

The Magic Pudding

Energee   2000

VHS

Bunyip Bluegum the koala forms the Noble Society of Puddin'Owners with penguin Sam Sawnoff and sailor Bill Barnacle, sworn to protect Albert the Magic Pudding from trouble. But Bunyip has a hidden motive — he has just discovered that he might not be an orphan after all, and he needs their

★★★★★★★★★★★★★★★★★★★★★★★★★★★★★★★★

Credit watching: A "Foley Artist" is responsible for adding noises like footsteps and squeaky shoes if the sound doesn't come out right on the film.

★★★★★★★★★★★★★★★★★★★★★★★★★★★★★★★★

help to find his missing parents. A zany film based on the famous Australian book by Norman Lindsay, but, as with all movie adaptations, the book is still better! So if you can't find this British film on TV, you can at least read the book! Listen for former Monty Python star John Cleese as the Magic Pudding.

 Star rating: ○○

Mary Poppins
Walt Disney Productions/Buena   1964
DVD; VHS

The Banks children advertise for a new nanny, and get a magical one who whisks them away to a cartoon land of penguins and tea on a magic carousel. Perhaps the best of the Disney musicals, with memorable songs, including "Supercalifragilisticexpialidocious," "A Spoonful of Sugar," and the Oscar-winning "Chim Chim Cher-ee." Listen out for Dick Van Dyke's accent — does he honestly think he sounds like a London chimney sweep?

  Star rating: ○○○○

Matilda
PG
TriStar Pictures   1996
DVD; VHS

Matilda is a gifted child sent to an academy run by the iron-willed Agatha Trunchbull. She uses her newfound super-powers to scare Trunchbull, so that Trunchbull's estranged stepdaughter Miss Honey can take over the school and treat everyone *nicely*. Extreme nastiness done to adults by children, so guaranteed to be a hit with all the kids in the family.

Star rating: ✪✪✪

Men in Black
PG-13
Columbia Pictures   1997
DVD; VHS

"Put up your hands and all of your flippers!" Agents K and J are Men in Black, in charge of policing crime among the earth's many alien inhabitants, who have been secretly blending in since the 1950s. Their latest mission — stopping alien runaway Edgar, who is plotting an interstellar incident involving a galaxy on "Orion's belt."

There are two DVDs, the excellent Collectors Edition (with "Making of," alternate scenes, artwork, etc.), and the superb Limited Edition, which includes your chance to edit several scenes yourself. Perhaps the best DVD released so far. Followed by *MIB2*, unreleased at time of writing.

  Star rating: ✪✪✪✪

Alien Invasion:
E.T. The Extra Terrestrial
Flight of the Navigator
*Batteries Not Included
Men in Black

THEME NIGHT

The Mighty Ducks

PG

Buena Vista Pictures Distribution, Inc.   1992
DVD; VHS

Lawyer Gordon Bombay is forced to coach the area's worst hockey team, even though he is haunted by childhood memories of losing the championship for his own school team. He brings the Mighty Ducks back to winning status until the finals, when he faces a team lead by his own former coach. Sports movies all seem to follow the same zero-to-hero template, but this is better than average. Unfortunately, the same cannot be said for the DVD, which simply forces some trailers down your gullet and then plays the film. There are also two sequels and, strangely, a *video* spin-off which calls itself *Mighty Ducks: The Movie*. As if things weren't confusing enough already!

Star rating: ✪✪✪

Mighty Morphin Power Rangers: The Movie

PG

Twentieth Century Fox Film Corp.   1995
DVD; VHS

Extraterrestrial mentor Zordon has trained six Californian teenagers to defend their hometown of Angel Grove from alien attacks. Hard-pressed by new enemy Ivan Ooze, the Power Rangers are transported to the distant world of Phados, where they gain new powers from the witch Dulcea, before returning to do battle with Ivan's ectomorphicons. This is the big movie spin-off of the long-running TV series — big in its day, but does anyone remember the Power Rangers now? If you do, then this is for you. The DVD version thoughtfully includes the sequel *Turbo: A Power Rangers Movie*, in which Divatox, the space pirate, plans to release the monstrous Maligore, who is trapped in a volcano. It's not very good, but as extras go, it's pretty massive.

Star rating: ✪✪

Monsters Inc.
Pixar/Walt Disney Pictures   2002
DVD; VHS

Monsters Inc. is the factory where scaring kids is just another job — kindly Mike and Sulley are just two of the ugly creatures who are ordered into kids' closets at night to scare them. That's how Monstropolis generates its power, but modern human kids are tough to scare, and times are getting harder. The trouble begins when a real human child accidentally comes through into Monstropolis, turning the tables on the lily-livered creatures (they only *look* scary) and rousing the anger of the fearsome Child Detection Agency. Great fun for all the family, from the people who brought you **Toy Story** — you'll get no complaints from the adults, who'll love it as much as you do.

 Star rating: ✪✪✪✪✪

Mouse Hunt
PG
Dreamworks Distribution L.L.C.   1997
DVD; VHS

String magnates Eric and Lars Smunts inherit a rundown house designed by a famous architect, which they intend to renovate and sell. But they are thwarted by its sole resident, a plucky mouse that refuses to move. Mad machines, cat-and-mouse action, and some painful stuff with traps make this a rodent version of **HOME ALONE**. The DVD includes several deleted scenes and cast biographies.

 Star rating: ✪✪✪✪

 During production on HARRY POTTER AND THE SORCERER'S STONE, studio documents referred to it as The Road to Thunder to keep out nosy journalists.

Mrs. Doubtfire
PG-13
Twentieth Century Fox Film Corp.   1993
DVD; VHS

Voice-over artist Daniel Hillard, played by Robin Williams, loses custody of his children to his ex-wife Miranda and decides to impersonate a middle-aged, female British housekeeper (Mrs. Doubtfire) to stay close to them. A funny comedy for older viewers, especially if they, too, are the victims of divorce, but a little close to the bone for youngsters — in Britain the film became the subject of a minor scandal when bad language was *added*. The DVD extras include many deleted scenes, the cartoon sequence we see Daniel working on, and a good director's commentary for the grown-ups — good value.

Star rating: ✪✪✪

Mulan
Buena Vista Pictures Distribution, Inc.   1998
DVD; VHS

When the Emperor calls for every family to send a soldier to fight off a Hun invasion, Mulan disguises herself as a man and goes in place of her aged father. Her ancestors send Mushu, a dragon, to look after her. to the excellent battle with the scary Huns (but I'll come clean, this is my favorite Disney cartoon, so I don't think you should be fast-forwarding at all!). Flabbergast adults by saying that some of the shot compositions remind you of Kurosawa movies and that the animation style seems to be influenced by Tang Dynasty art. Look for hidden Mickey Mouses on a railing beside steps and in the middle of charging troops. The extras on the DVD, however, are pathetic.

  Star rating: ✪✪✪✪

Girl Power:
Mulan
Kiki's Delivery Service
The New Adventures of Pippi
    Longstocking
Matilda
The Journey of Natty Gann

The Muppet Movie
Associated Film Distributors   1979
DVD; VHS

The story of how the muppets first came together. Kermit the Frog gathers his friends for his rise to

Hollywood fame, avoiding the unwelcome attentions of a restaurant owner who specializes in frogs' legs. Great fun for children and adults alike (albeit for different reasons). to songs "Movin'Right Along" and the Oscar-nominated "Rainbow Connection," though they are only two of several good songs. The DVD extras include camera tests (13 minutes of random scenes designed to test the suitability of the muppets in certain settings) and some brief commercial-length "Muppetisms" — better than nothing, but not much better than nothing.

 Star rating: ✪✪✪

The Muppets Take Manhattan
TriStar Pictures   1984
DVD; VHS

The Muppets decide to take their theater production *Manhattan Melodies* on the road — all the way to Manhattan itself, home of Broadway. But they arrive to find that nobody wants to put their play on, while Kermit loses his memory and finds a job in an all-frog advertising agency. One of the weaker entries in the Muppet movie series, though the DVD extras do include a few choice quotes from Muppet creator Jim Henson.

 Star rating: ✪✪

Muppet Treasure Island
Buena Vista Pictures Distribution, Inc.   1995
DVD; VHS

"Right now I'm somewhere between bed-wetting and a near-death experience." Captain Smollett (Kermit the Frog) and his associate Benjamina

Gunn (Miss Piggy) vie with the bad guy Long John Silver (Tim Curry, not a muppet) to find buried treasure. ▶ to the moment when being cooped up on the ship gives everyone the feeling of (and song of) "Cabin Fever."

  Star rating: ✪✪✪

Muppets from Space
Columbia Pictures   1999
DVD; VHS

"May the fish be with you." Gonzo becomes convinced that he is really an alien, while Miss Piggy gets a job as the first pig to have her own talk show. The extras on the DVD are very good for once — a live video commentary (with two muppets and the director sharing production gossip), music video, and hilarious deleted scenes. This is the most recent of the Muppet movies — there is also a Muppet version of **A CHRISTMAS CAROL**.

  Star rating: ✪✪✪

My Little Pony — The Movie
De Laurentiis Entertainment Group   1986
VHS

In the Volcano of Doom, Hydia the witch and her daughters make smooze to cover the little ponies' valley. The ponies go in search of the Flutter Ponies to help them. "My Little Ponies" were the world's most boring toys — multicolored statues of horses whose hair you could brush. Like them, this film is about as much fun as a trip to the dentist. There are many other videos comprising episodes of the

TV series, but they are only likely to be used as a form of parental punishment.

Star rating: ✪

Horse Sense:
NATIONAL VELVET
BLACK BEAUTY
THE BLACK STALLION
MY LITTLE PONY

THEME NIGHT

My Neighbor Totoro
Fiftieth Street Films   1993
VHS

Mei and Satsuki stay in the country with their father while their mother is recuperating in the hospital. They scare dust-bunnies from the house and meet the local Totoros, fat furry spirits that only children can see, who play in the forest and ride in a Catbus. One of the best children's films ever made. Confuse your parents by informing them it was written by Hayao Miyazaki, a man tired of the good-versus-evil conflicts of Disney cartoons, who decided it was time to just have fun.

 Star rating: ✪✪✪✪✪

Namu: The Killer Whale
MGM   1966
US/VHS

Predictable tale about an orca (unhelpfully referred to by many people as a "killer whale") which is captured and trained to perform for humans. Unbelieveably, while it may look like a rip-off of **Free Willy**, it is actually based on a true story and twenty years older.

Star rating: ✪✪

Napoleon and Samantha
Walt Disney Productions/Buena   1972
DVD; VHS

Children Napoleon and Samantha go on the run with their "pet," a fearsome circus lion. Watch out for a very young Jodie Foster (**Freaky Friday**) and Michael Douglas in this 1970s Disney live-action movie. The extras seem in a time warp, too: There's absolutely nothing added on this DVD.

Star rating: ✪✪✪

National Velvet
MGM Film Company   1944
DVD; VHS

English girl Velvet Brown names her horse Pie (Pirate) and plans to win the Grand National racing event. But though she begins training Pie, she knows that she doesn't have the money to enter the race. The ultimate horse-racing movie for girls — better this than the woeful remake, *International Velvet*. Looks like the people who made the DVD were strapped for cash, too — no extras worth speaking of. There was also a TV series, with Lori Martin replacing Elizabeth Taylor in the lead role.

Star rating: ✪✪✪✪

Never Cry Wolf
PG
Walt Disney Productions/Buena   1983
DVD; VHS

Tyler the biologist is sent into the extreme north of
Canada. His mission? To prove that wolves are
destroying the herds of caribou. But he develops a
new respect for the creatures he is supposed to be
studying when a local Inuit teaches him about the
wolf way of life. Perhaps a little slow for younger
viewers, but a surprise treat for older ones — and
it's not every day that you see a Disney film in
which the lead character lives on mouse stew.
Even though a "Making of" was made, and this is
based on a *true* story, there shamefully are no
extras on the DVD.

Star rating: ✪✪✪✪

The Neverending Story
PG
Warner Bros.   1984
DVD; VHS

After his mother dies, Bastian Balthasar Bux spends
most of his time with his nose buried in a book,
reading about the magical world of Fantasia. But
the Childlike Empress of Fantasia needs his help
and drags him into the book to save her world
from Nothingness. The DVD includes the unrelated
bonus cartoon "Box Office Bunny," which was
shown before the film in movie theaters.

Star rating: ✪✪✪

The Neverending Story II: The Next Chapter

PG

Warner Bros.   1990

DVD; VHS

Fantasia is now threatened by Emptiness, and the Childlike Empress recalls Bastian to help her again, with his friends Falkor (a dragon that looks like a dog), mountain creature Rockbiter, and Nimbly the bird. He unwittingly sells his soul to the evil sorceress Xayide, but can call on Atreyu, the hero of the Book, to help him save the day. The first film stopped halfway through the original book, so although it is really just the rest of the original story, it still feels like a bad case of sequelitis.

Star rating: ✪✪

 Victor and Hugo, two of the gargoyles in THE HUNCHBACK OF NOTRE DAME, are named after the novelist Victor Hugo, who wrote the original book.

The Neverending Story III

Miramax Films   1996

VHS

Back on Earth, Bastian has to deal with the arrival of his new stepsister Nicole and the unwelcome attentions of school bullies. He escapes to Fantasia, but leaves the Book behind — when it falls into the hands of the bullies, it causes chaos. The Childlike Empress orders him back, but he accidentally takes his magical friends with him. ▶ to the song "Born to be Wild." If you like that, then you can probably endure the rest of this film. Also ▶ every time Bastian and Nicole are on-screen arguing — stick to the fantasy creatures. There is also a *Tales from the Neverending Story* TV series.

Star rating: ✪

The New Adventures of Pippi Longstocking
Columbia Pictures Entertainment   1988
DVD; VHS

Red-haired Pippi is the daughter of an angel and a pirate, and she has enough super-powers to fight crime like a regular superhero . . . except she doesn't. Accompanied by her talking horse and pet monkey, she sets up home next door to the straight-laced Annika and Tommy, causing trouble not only for them, but also for cheating corporations, interfering social workers, and the inmates of an orphanage. Good fun, especially for girls tired of damsels in distress. Extras are limited to a few production notes. There is also a cartoon version, called just plain *Pippi Longstocking*, and several earlier feature and TV versions, all based on the original Swedish books.

Star rating: ✪✪✪

The Nightmare Before Christmas
PG
Buena Vista Pictures Distribution, Inc.   1993
DVD; VHS

In the spooky Halloween town, Jack Skellington the Pumpkin King is bored with the same old thing. Instead, he decides to run Christmas for a year, turning it from a festival of joy to a carnival of fear and terror. And about time, too. A refreshingly creepy and unpleasant antidote to all those other Christmas movies. The Special Edition DVD contains a "Making of," deleted scenes, and two shorts — *Vincent* and *Frankenweenie*.

  Star rating: ✪✪✪

THEME NIGHT

Fright Night:
JURASSIC PARK
WATCHER IN THE WOODS
THE NIGHTMARE BEFORE CHRISTMAS
BAMBI

Old Yeller
Walt Disney Productions/Buena   1958
VHS

Heartrending tale of Arliss, a young boy who adopts a stray dog and turns him into the family pet. But when Arliss is attacked by wild boars, Yeller catches rabies defending him. A miserable weepy film, useful only for tormenting adults. There is also a sequel: *Savage Sam*.

 Star rating: ✪✪✪

Oliver & Company
Buena Vista Pictures Distribution, Inc.   1988
DVD; VHS

Oliver the orphaned cat meets a group of stray dogs led by the artful Dodger. He is eventually adopted by a human girl, Jenny, but her pedigreed cat Georgette gets jealous. Kidnapped by the evil

Sikes, Oliver must rely on his newfound friends to save the day. ▶️ to Dodger's musical number "Why Should I Worry?" And look out for a Mickey Mouse watch. The DVD includes two doggie-themed short cartoons and two sing-along sections.

 Star rating: ✪✪✪

101 Dalmatians (animated film)
Walt Disney Productions/Buena   1961
DVD; VHS

When human beings Roger and Anita fall in love and get married, their dogs do, too! Dalmatians Pongo and Perdita have 15 cute little puppies, but the dogs are stolen by the henchmen of Cruella De Vil, a bad woman who wants a coat made of Dalmatian fur. The dogs rescue their offspring, along with 84 other stolen puppies. Packed with golden moments (and see if you can see the Mickey Mouse outlines hidden in spots and windows). Hardly any extras on the DVD at all — Cruella De Video perhaps! There was also a belated follow-up on video only — *101 Dalmatians Christmas* — in which Cruella De Vil fires her servant on Christmas Eve and is then visited by several ghosts — yes, it's a rip-off of CHRISTMAS CAROL.

  Star rating: ✪✪✪✪

101 Dalmatians (live-action)
Buena Vista Pictures Distribution, Inc.   1996
DVD; VHS

When human beings Roger and Anita fall in love and get married . . . *hang on* . . . yes, this is a remake of the earlier film, but done with real people and real dogs. The last section plays like

HOME ALONE, but with dogs. Impress adults by saying it's because both films were written by the same guy, John Hughes. Another DVD with no extras worth speaking of — the *real* criminals aren't just stealing puppies anymore, that's for sure.

 Star rating: ✪✪✪

102 Dalmatians (live-action)
Buena Vista Pictures Distribution, Inc.   2000
DVD; VHS

After the events of *101 Dalmatians*, Cruella De Vil has been cured! Now a dog lover, she is released from prison and takes over a rundown dog sanctuary. But Cruella doesn't stay good for long — the chimes of Big Ben restore her to her old self. Now she wants 99 Dalmatians to make a coat, and *three* more for a hood. But Dipstick, one of the original puppies from *101*, now has Dalmatian puppies of his own, and he's determined to stop her, with a little human help. Listen for Waddlesworth, a silly parrot who thinks he's a rottweiler, but can translate between the dogs and the humans. Unavoidable *awww* factor in the form of Oddball, a Dalmatian with no spots. DVD extras

★★★★★★★★★★★★★★★★★★★★★★★★★★★★★★
★ **Credit watching:** A "Key Grip" is in charge ★
★ of moving stuff around the set, putting up ★
★ scaffolding, cranes, and what have you. ★
★ The "dolly grip" is the person in charge of ★
★ the "dolly" — a camera on tracks used to ★
★ film people on the move ("tracking shots"). ★
★★★★★★★★★★★★★★★★★★★★★★★★★★★★★★

include a deleted scene, bloopers, puppy auditions, and a Cruella costume-design game, as well as commentaries for grown-up film buffs. Much more like it!

Star rating: ✪✪✪

One of Our Dinosaurs Is Missing
Walt Disney Productions/Buena   1975
VHS

Escaping from China with the formula for "Lotus X," Lord Southmere hides the microfilm inside the bones of one of the dinosaurs at the National History Museum. Spies decide to steal the entire skeleton, but are thwarted by a group of plucky nannies. If you were expecting **JURASSIC PARK**, you'll be disappointed. This dinosaur is very dead, and so are large parts of the film.

Star rating: ✪✪

The Pagemaster
Twentieth Century Fox Film Corp.   1994
VHS

Richard Tyler is scared of absolutely everything and takes refuge from a storm in a library. Though he only wants to use the phone, he is dragged by the librarian Mr. Dewey into the world of books, where he is transformed into a cartoon version of himself. This sounds a lot more interesting than it really is, and you are hereby warned — any grown-up in hearing distance will start lecturing you about how you really ought to be reading books instead of watching films about them. And in this particular case, they may be right! Unless you particularly want to see Macaulay

Culkin (from **Home Alone**) and Christopher Lloyd (from **Back to the Future**), ⊘ to the cartoony parts.

Star rating: ❂❂

The Parent Trap
PG
Buena Vista Pictures Distribution, Inc.   1998
DVD; VHS

Annie and Hallie meet at a summer camp, where they discover that they are twins, secretly separated during their parents' divorce. They decide to swap places and reunite their parents, though their father Nick is already falling in love with a would-be wicked stepmother. Don't listen to the adults. By all *children's* accounts, this new version seems to go down better than the original Disney version starring Hayley Mills as the twins. If you get any trouble from the grown-ups, stump them by revealing that the "original" they cherish so much was actually a remake of a British movie, *Twice Upon a Time*, and *that* was based on a German book.

Star rating: ❂❂❂

Paulie
PG
DreamWorks Distribution L.L.C.   1998
DVD; VHS

Paulie, a parrot that can really talk, has a series of adventures as he passes from owner to owner — a lonely widow, a Mexican singer, and a thief. But it's Paulie's original owner, a little girl whose stutter he helps to cure, who remains in his heart.

118

Touching and funny, but though it would dearly like to be **BABE** with feathers, it's not quite as good as that. The DVD includes production notes and cast/crew bios — better than nothing, but not *that* much better.

Star rating: ✪✪✪

Peanuts Holiday Collection
United Media   1974
DVD; VHS

Charlie Brown and his beagle Snoopy in three seasonal adventures (made for TV): *It's The Great Pumpkin, Charlie Brown; A Charlie Brown Thanksgiving;* and *A Charlie Brown Christmas.* The three-disc set (why couldn't they put them all on one!?) also contains some bonus material — *You're Not Elected, Charlie Brown, It's Christmas Time Again, Charlie Brown,* and the historical cartoon *The Mayflower Voyages.* See also **SNOOPY COME HOME.**

Star rating: ✪✪✪

The Pebble and the Penguin
Metro-Goldwyn-Mayer, Inc.   1995
DVD; VHS

Hubie, a shy penguin, wishes he had the perfect stone to impress local penguinette Marina. He finds what he needs in the center of a meteorite, but fights with his love-rival, Drake, and is captured by humans. Washed up on a South Sea island with his associate Rocko, he has to get home before Marina agrees to Drake's suit and he loses her forever. Some nice songs from Barry Manilow, but not that great a movie. Annoy adults by asking why only Drake has teeth. No worthwhile extras on the DVD.

 Star rating: ✪✪✪

All the adult scenes in BIG were rehearsed with "young Josh" (actor David Moscow) playing the Tom Hanks role, so Hanks could see how a real child would behave in each situation.

Peter Pan
Walt Disney Productions/Buena   1952
DVD; VHS

Peter Pan, a boy who has never grown up, whisks Wendy Darling and her siblings away to Never Land, where they rescue an Indian princess and fight pirates led by the evil Captain Hook. ⏩ to "Never Smile at a Crocodile," which is handy advice for us all. Watch for the scene where Wendy is splashed by the mermaids — her hair seems to go red briefly. The DVD includes a brief "Making of" and three sing-along songs. See also **HOOK**. A sequel, *Return to Never Land*, was released in 2002.

 Star rating: ✪✪✪✪

Pete's Dragon
Walt Disney Productions/Buena   1977
DVD; VHS

Pete is on the run from his parents, accompanied by his dragon friend Elliott. He finds a place to stay at a lighthouse in Maine but is soon pursued once more by the evil Dr. Terminus. A combination of cartoon and live-action in the spirit of Mary Poppins, the film comes loaded with songs, including "Bill of Sale" and "Room for Everyone." The DVD has nothing on it — you might as well save money and get the VHS.

 Star rating: ✪✪✪

The Phantom Tollbooth
MGM Film Company   1969
VHS

Bored schoolboy Milo comes home to find a tollbooth in his room. He gets into a toy car and drives through it, into a cartoon world, where he must rescue the princesses Rhyme and Reason. Plenty of songs like "Don't Say There's Nothing to Do in the Doldrums" and (my favorite) "Rhyme and Reason Reign Again," but likely to look too dated for older viewers. Milo was played by Butch Patrick, better known as Eddie Munster.

 Star rating: ✪✪✪

Pinocchio
Walt Disney Productions/Buena   1940
DVD; VHS

Pinocchio is a wooden puppet that desperately wishes to be a real boy. The Blue Fairy offers to make his wish come true, but only if he learns the difference between right and wrong. Widely regarded as one of the best of the Disney cartoons — the Oscar-winning song "When You Wish upon a Star" was so popular it became the Disney theme song. Nothing on the DVD — where

121

was the distributor's conscience on the day that came out? There are many other versions of the story, from as far back as 1911, with the most recent to date in 2002.

  Star rating: ✪✪✪✪

Pocahontas
Buena Vista Pictures Distribution, Inc.   1995
DVD; VHS

Algonquin princess Pocahontas falls in love with John Smith, an English adventurer who has arrived in the Americas in search of gold. When things turn frosty between the newcomers and the local inhabitants, it is only the love of Pocahontas and John that can prevent the onset of war. The song "Colors of the Wind" won an Oscar. Annoy adults by asking why Smith's ship is flying the Union Jack when Britain didn't use that flag for another century. The DVD contains a read-along section, a trivia game, and two music videos.

 Star rating: ✪✪✪

Pocahontas 2: Journey to a New World
Walt Disney   1998
DVD; VHS

Pocahontas hears that John Smith has died back home, and sails to England to meet with the king in an attempt to keep the peace. But her enemy Ratcliffe still has plans for the Americas and needs to be stopped. Listen for Donal Gibson, who takes over his brother Mel's role as John Smith.

Impress adults by pointing out that 17th-century London was unlikely to have had gaslights; also that Pocahontas is based on a true story, but in the real world, she came back to England *with* John Smith and died soon after in Kent. Nothing worthwhile on the DVD.

 Star rating: ✪✪

Pokémon, The First Movie
Warner Bros.   1999
DVD; VHS

Mewtwo, a genetically engineered monster, escapes from the lab where he was created and tries to take over the world. He does so by organizing a trap on New Island, where Pokémon trainer Ash and his friends are going to a tournament. It's a bit weird that the grand finale tells us how bad it is to fight all the time, but that's *all they ever do* in the TV series! Plenty of extras, though, including a commentary, music video, and history of Pokémon on the DVD.

Star rating: ✪

Pokémon The Movie 2000
Warner Bros.   2000
DVD; VHS

Pokémon trainer Ash Ketchum discovers that he is the Chosen One, who must find and unite three spheres to prevent the end of the world. This is approaching because the evil Pokémon collector Lawrence III has abducted the three mega-Pokémon — Moltres, Zapdos, and Articuno from their island hideaway. Awful, awful, awful. Extras include a music video and, surprise surprise, an ad for **POKÉMON 3**.

Star rating: ✪

THEME NIGHT

Fight Night:
BUGSY MALONE
HOME ALONE
MIGHTY MORPHIN POWER RANGERS
POKÉMON

Pokémon The Movie 3
Warner Bros.   2001
DVD; VHS

While her widowed father goes in search of the mystical Unown monster, Molly befriends a lionlike creature called Entei, who realizes she wants a mother. Entei kidnaps Ash Ketchum's own mother and brings her to Molly's crystal home, and the Pokémon trainers must go there to snatch her back. Will the madness never end? The DVD includes the "Johto Poké-rap," a commentary, and fact files.

Star rating: ✪

The Prince of Egypt
PG
DreamWorks Distribution L.L.C.   1998
DVD; VHS

The Pharaoh Seti orders the death of Israelite children, but one mother hides her son, Moses, by the river. He is found by the Pharaoh's daughter and brought up as her own child. But he is forced to hide when he tries to protect a slave and ends up killing an overseer. A lavish production of the Biblical story, complete with computer-enhanced plagues of Egypt and the parting of the Red Sea. to the chariot race. The opening song, "Deliver Us," is the best, but "When You Believe" was the one that won an Oscar. You get the chance to hear it in 28 different languages as one of the DVD extras, which also includes a commentary and three behind-the-scenes documentaries.

 Star rating: ✪✪✪

The Princess Bride
PG
Twentieth Century Fox Film Corp.   1987
DVD; VHS

Buttercup, a beautiful girl, is betrothed to the evil prince Humperdinck. Her true love, Westley, accompanied by a giant and a Spanish swordsman, fights to get her back. By turns funny, action-packed, and romantic, this is the ideal film for all the family. Little chance of ▶ing here although Westley's cliff-top sword fight with Inigo rivals the best of Errol Flynn. The standard DVD version is bare of extras, though the "Special Edition" is loaded with behind-the-scenes footage, commentaries, and a new anniversary documentary.

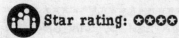 **Star rating: ✪✪✪✪**

Quest for Camelot

Warner Bros.   1998

DVD; VHS

Knight's daughter Kayley joins forces with a hermit called Garrett in the search for King Arthur's magic sword Excalibur, which was stolen by the griffin that killed her father. En route, they team up with the two-headed dragon "Devon and Cornwall" and discover the theft was part of the evil Sir Ruber's plot to seize Camelot for himself. So-so, but listen for the songs — when Kayley starts to sing, she transforms into Andrea Corr (of the Corrs), and her mother, Juliana, suddenly develops a singing voice provided by Celine Dion. The DVD includes a "Making of," a music video, and a short bonus cartoon featuring the same characters.

 Star rating: ✪✪

The Railway Children

Universal City Studios, Inc.   1971

VHS

A well-to-do Edwardian family is forced to move to Yorkshire when the father is imprisoned on trumped-up charges. The children play on and around the railway and eventually discover the chance to help their father out. A sweet little film, piled high with tea sets and frocks, for those who like that sort of thing (i.e., period drama). Jenny Agutter, who played

★★★★★★★★★★★★★★★★★★★★★★★★★★★★★★
★ **Credit watching:** A "Best Boy" is the chief ★
★ electrician's assistant. (Some "best boys" ★
★ are actually girls.) ★
★★★★★★★★★★★★★★★★★★★★★★★★★★★★★★

Bobbie in the original, returns to play her own mother in the 2000 remake. If you can't find the video (it's only available in the United Kingdom), you can always read the book, by E. Nesbit.

Star rating: ✪✪✪

Recess: School's Out
Buena Vista Pictures Distribution, Inc. 2000
VHS

Ten-year-old T. J. is convinced he's facing a boring summer vacation when all his friends head off to camp without him. But then he discovers a sinister plot to end school vacations forever and rounds up his old gang (and some helpful teachers) to save the day. A movie-length spin-off from the TV cartoon series, featuring T. J. teaming up with his old nemesis, Principal Prickly, in order to defeat a greater evil.

Star rating: ✪✪✪

The Rescuers
Walt Disney Productions/Buena 1977
VHS

Mouse Rescue Aid Society members Bernard and Miss Bianca must rescue Penny, a young girl held captive in the Devil's Bayou by the evil Madame

Frock Schlock:
A LITTLE PRINCESS
LITTLE WOMEN
THE RAILWAY CHILDREN

THEME NIGHT

Medusa. to Orville the albatross, a one-man airline, complete with his own sardine-can cabin.

 Star rating: ✪✪✪

When STAR WARS: EPISODE VI — RETURN OF THE JEDI was being made, studio documents referred to it as a horror movie called *Blue Harvest*, in order to put snooping journalists off the scent.

The Rescuers Down Under

Buena Vista Pictures Distribution, Inc.   1990
DVD; VHS

Belated sequel to the original, in which Bernard and Miss Bianca are dispatched to Australia to rescue Cody, a boy who has been kidnapped by evil poacher McLeach. A double mission follows, to save Cody and the eagle's eggs he is protecting. Look for hidden Mickey Mouses in the outline of the eggs, and in the shape of a bush. The DVD includes a trivia game and a read-along section.

Star rating: ✪✪

Escape from the KIDS section #3:
Old-School Comedies
Can't bear another "funny" movie written with kids in mind? Then try *Bringing Up Baby*. *Way Out West* or *His Girl Friday*. Or watch *A Night at the Opera* and tell your parents it turned you into a Marxist (brother!).

128

The Return of the King

Warner Bros.   1979
US/DVD

Frodo and his assistant Sam must throw the Ring of Doom into the fires of a volcano to save the world, though they are being tracked by Gollum, the Ring's last-but-one owner. After the cartoon version of **Lord of the Rings** came to a sudden halt halfway, the Rankin-Bass animation studio made this fix-up to tell the rest of the story on television, with the same cutesy look at the same studio's earlier **Hobbit**. Though this does complete the story, it's a real disappointment. Better to wait for the end of the live-action movie series in 2003.

Star rating: ✪✪

Return to Oz

PG
Walt Disney Productions/Buena   1985
DVD; VHS

Back in Kansas, Dorothy pines for her friends. But when a doctor tries to treat her with electricity, she is transported back to Oz, where she finds the land ruled by the evil Nome King, and her old friends turned to stone. She joins forces with Tik-Tok (the clockwork one-man army), Jack Pumpkinhead, and Gump to save the land again, but the new witch Mombie wants her head! Much darker and scarier than the original film, this sequel was made nearly fifty years later. The DVD includes an eleven-minute interview with Dorothy actress Fairuza Balk, now much older and even prettier.

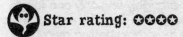 **Star rating: ✪✪✪✪**

Richie Rich

PG

Warner Bros.   1994

VHS

Richie is the richest boy in the world, left in charge
of the United Tools company when his parents are
missing. He needs the help of inventor Professor
Keenbean to save them from the evil Van Dough,
a businessman who covets Richie's riches for
himself. Perhaps the last "kid" movie made by
HOME ALONE star Macaulay Culkin. Watch out for a
mysteriously self-altering coffee-stain on someone's
clothes. There is also the predictable video
follow-up, *Richie Rich's Christmas Wish.*

Star rating: ✪✪

The Road to El Dorado

DreamWorks Distribution L.L.C.   2000

DVD; VHS

Feckless con men Tulio and Miguel use a stolen
map to find the fabled South American city of El
Dorado. The local people worship the con men as
gods, except one local girl, Chel, who promises to
help them steal the gold if they will take her away
with them. But Spanish invaders are getting nearer,
and high-priest Tzekel-Kan keeps on asking the
boys to perform miracles. High points include
Tzekel-Kan's attacking robot-monster and the boys
cheating at a game by using their pet armadillo
for a ball. There's a lot of fun for grown-ups, too,
but younger viewers might get confused. Minor
kissing stuff is well handled and over with quickly,
and the characters strangely sing only one song
themselves, while Elton John sings the rest. But it's a
nice change to see the crooks getting away with

it, even if deep down they have hearts of . . .
well . . . gold.

  Star rating: ✪✪✪✪

Robin Hood
Walt Disney Productions/Buena   1973
DVD; VHS

Robin Hood (a fox outlaw) opposes the minions of
the evil (and stupid) King John, a feckless lion left in
charge of England while his brother, King Richard,
is fighting in the Crusades. One of my favorite
Disney cartoons, but strangely disliked by a lot of
grown-ups — even though the songs are better,
the jokes are funnier, and there are plenty of sword
fights. There's no pleasing some people. The DVD
includes a read-along storybook, trivia game, and
a Mickey Mouse short *Olden Days*.

  Star rating: ✪✪✪✪

Rock-A-Doodle
Samuel Goldwyn Company   1991
DVD; VHS

Chanticleer, a rooster that fails to bring up the sun
(as is his duty) is cast out of the farm and heads for
Las Vegas, where he gets a job as a lounge singer.
Human boy Edmond is turned into a cat and goes
to beg Chanticleer to come back before the
world is plunged into eternal darkness. Don't panic
when it starts as live-action, ⏩ through the
beginning until you get to the cartoon part, but
even then, the songs somehow seem a little dull.

 Star rating: ✪✪

131

Rugrats in Paris — The Movie
Paramount Pictures Corp.   2000
DVD; VHS

French money-grubber Coco La Bouche has Chuckie's dad wrapped around her little finger, and the Rugrats must expose her plans before she marries him and ensnares him forever. Luckily, they are in Paris for the repair of the Reptar robot, and they steal it to help them. Keep an eye on Chuckie's teddy bear — the bite mark on its ear keeps changing sides. If anything, this is better than *The Rugrats Movie*, and the DVD keeps up the pace, with a documentary, two alternate endings, a music video, and games.

 Star rating: ✪✪✪

The Rugrats Movie
Paramount Pictures Corp.   1998
DVD; VHS

Tommy Pickles is ousted from his mother's affections by Dylan, her new baby. After "borrowing" his father's new invention with his friends Chuckie, Phil, Lil, and Betty, he tries to take Dylan back to the hospital to restore everything to normality. By turns funny and weepy, and a real treat for anyone who likes *The Rugrats* TV series. Watch for Stu's propellers when he's flying — they fall off but seem to magically reattach themselves. The DVD includes the bonus cartoon *Catdog*.

 Star rating: ✪✪✪

Scooby Doo on Zombie Island

Warner Bros   1998

DVD; VHS

The occupants of the Mystery Machine find themselves on Zombie Island, haunted by the ghost of Moonscar the pirate. Who could it possibly be, and will they get away with it without those meddling kids? A little scary for the very young (but what do you expect? — it *is* a ghost story). The extras include a "featurette" which is more like a big ad, a trivia game, and some trailers for other Scooby releases. Your parents will be surprisingly engrossed — they were kids once, too, you know.

 Star rating: ✪✪✪✪

The Secret Garden

Warner Bros.   1993

DVD; VHS

After she loses her parents in an earthquake in India, Mary is sent to live at her uncle's mansion in the north of England. There she discovers a locked, walled garden, tended by local boy

★★★★★★★★★★★★★★★★★★★★★★★★★★★★★
★ **Credit watching:** A "Set Dresser" ★
★ decorates the place where the film is ★
★ made. When historical films are shot "on ★
★ location" (that is, in a real place, not a ★
★ studio), this can involve hiding modern ★
★ things like TV aerials and satellite dishes. ★
★★★★★★★★★★★★★★★★★★★★★★★★★★★★★

Dickon, where she takes her disabled cousin Colin without her uncle's knowledge. Not much of interest on the DVD, except the film itself, which is charming enough. An earlier version, made chiefly in black-and-white in 1949, was filmed in America. This version was filmed in Yorkshire, though the garden itself was built in a studio using 17,000 flowers!

Star rating: ✪✪✪

According to the animators on ALADDIN, the face of the evil Jafar was partly modeled on that of Nancy Reagan, wife of the U.S. president.

The Secret of Nimh
United Artists   1982
DVD; VHS

Mrs. Brisby, a mouse, and her four children are in danger because the local human farmer intends to plow a field right over their home. With one of her children very ill, she seeks help from the local rats, who reveal that they were once experimental subjects at the National Institute for Mental Health. No worthwhile extras on the DVD — do they think we're lab rats, too? Listen for a *very* young Shannen Doherty (*Beverly Hills 90210*) as Teresa.

 Star rating: ✪✪✪

134

The Secret of Nimh 2: Timmy to the Rescue

MGM Home Entertainment, Inc.   1998
DVD; VHS

Timmy (son of Mr. and Mrs. Brisby) heads out to Thorn Valley, where he is told that a number of mice are still missing, presumed dead. So he rescues them, hoping to find his would-be girlfriend's parents among them. A truly awful sequel to the original, and followed by another lackluster cash-in — *The Secret of Nimh 3: The Beginning*. Save yourself the agony and just watch the original three times. The DVD is, as might be expected, completely free of extras.

 Star rating: ✪

The Seventh Voyage of Sinbad

Columbia Pictures Industries   1958
DVD; VHS

Princess Parisa has been shrunk to **THUMBELINA** proportions by the evil wizard Sokurah. Sinbad must go on a quest to save her. ⏩ to the stunning fights with a giant cyclops, armored skeletons, a fire-breathing dragon, and a two-headed roc. What's even more amazing is that they were all made the old-fashioned way, with stop-motion animation — no computer graphics. The DVD extras include a documentary about Ray Harryhausen, a featurette about his Dynamation animation technique, trailers for other Harryhausen films, and some cast and crew bios. Seventh heaven!

Star rating: ✪✪✪

The Shaggy D.A.
Walt Disney Productions/Buena   1976
VHS

American lawyer Wilby Daniels keeps on turning into a sheepdog every time someone reads the inscription on a magic ring. He schemes to keep it secret, while avoiding the dog catcher! And yes, that's Dean Jones again, who would have more doggy difficulty in BEETHOVEN. A treat for the younger ones.

Star rating: ✪✪✪

Shipwrecked!
Warner Bros.   1978
VHS

Widowed father Travis, his two daughters, and Kelly the reporter (and obvious love interest) are attempting to sail around the world, but are shipwrecked on a remote Alaskan island that has no human inhabitants, but many wild animals. They try to catch salmon, they rescue a caribou, and try to build a boat to escape . . . and all the while, you will feel the will to live slowly sapping away, until you wonder what's on TV.

Star rating: ✪

Short Circuit
PG
TriStar Pictures   1986
DVD; VHS

Experimental robot Number Five suddenly develops intelligence. Refusing to perform the military functions for which he was built, he adopts animal lover Stephanie and proceeds to help her around the house. to the time he tries to make her breakfast! Look out for the moment when one of the crew members can be seen in Stephanie's mirror — oops! The DVD includes a good commentary, two behind-the-scenes featurettes, and interviews with some of the crew.

Star rating: ❂❂❂

Jules and Verne, Doc Brown's children in BACK TO THE FUTURE PART III, are named after Jules Verne, the 19th-century novelist who wrote *The Time Machine*.

Short Circuit II
PG
TriStar Pictures   1988
DVD; VHS

Now calling himself Johnny Five, the robot heads off to the big city to help his inventor, where he accidentally gets mixed up in a bank robbery. A disappointment after the first film. The extras comprise a rather pathetic set of interviews with the actors — not really worth it, just like the film.

Star rating: ❂

Shrek
PG
DreamWorks Distribution L.L.C.   2001
DVD; VHS

Shrek the ogre is intensely annoyed when his swamp is overrun by banished fairy-tale characters.

Accompanied by his wisecracking sidekick Donkey the donkey, he agrees to rescue bad-guy Farquaad's bride-to-be, Princess Fiona, from a fire-breathing dragon, but finds himself falling in love with her. A very funny film, lampooning Disney's fairy tales and showcasing incredible computer animation. Watch for the scene where Shrek walks out of a sunflower field — how come he's already managed to get an armful of corn and an onion?

  Star rating: ✪✪✪✪

Sleeping Beauty
Walt Disney Productions/Buena   1959
VHS

Maleficent the wicked fairy puts a curse on Princess Aurora at her christening, which she wasn't invited to. At age sixteen, Aurora pricks her finger on a spinning wheel and falls into a deep sleep that only a kiss from her true love can break. Maleficent also imprisons Prince Phillip to prevent him from rescuing Sleeping Beauty. When the good fairies help him escape, Malifecent turns into a fearsome dragon. Younger viewers will find this scarier than your average Disney. Watch for the three fairies having tea — Merryweather brings out biscuits shaped like Mickey Mouse!

Star rating: ✪✪✪

Small Soldiers
PG
DreamWorks Distribution L.L.C.   1998
DVD; VHS

Toy seller's son Alan gets a delivery of the new Commando Elite toys, which have been secretly fitted with military computer chips. The toys run amok and declare war on the Gorgonites, peace-loving alien toys. Look in the container behind the toy store for a puppet that looks like Gizmo, one of the creatures in the same director's earlier *Gremlins*. The DVD extras include bloopers, deleted scenes, and some behind-the-scenes footage.

Star rating: ✪✪✪

Snoopy Come Home
United Media   1972
VHS

Charlie Brown's pet beagle, Snoopy, learns that his original owner, Lila, is in the hospital. He sneaks off to see her with his friend Woodstock and, when she asks him to stay with her, he says his farewells to the old gang. A bittersweet tale from the people who gave you the **PEANUTS HOLIDAY COLLECTION**.

     Star rating: ✪✪✪✪

Snow White and the Seven Dwarfs
Walt Disney Productions/Buena   1937
DVD; VHS

When the wicked queen discovers that her stepdaughter Snow White is more beautiful than she will ever be, she orders her to be killed. Abandoned in the forest, Snow White meets seven dwarfs (Doc, Happy, Sleepy, Sneezy, Bashful, Grumpy, Dopey), and lives in safety with them . . . until the day the queen arrives in disguise, bearing a poisoned apple. The first Disney cartoon feature, and some might say the best. The DVD is utterly loaded with extras (as is the video), including missing scenes, a virtual tour of the castle, scenes from the premiere, interviews, sing-along sequences, a game, and a "Making of." As DVDs go, it could well be one of the fairest of them all.

 Star rating: ✪✪✪✪✪

 When he wrote the original novel of THE BLACK STALLION in 1941, author Walter Farley was still a teenager himself.

The Snowman
Children's Circle   1982
DVD; VHS

A snowman comes to life and takes the boy who built him on a magical flight around the world, before the sun rises and the snows start to melt. A beautiful short animated film — little to ⊙ through as it's only 23 minutes long. The extras appear to have melted away on the DVD, although it is bundled with the inferior cartoon *Father Christmas*, by the same team.

  Star rating: ✪✪✪✪

The Sound of Music
Twentieth Century Fox Film Corp.   1965
DVD; VHS

Maria is a young governess employed to care for the motherless children of Captain von Trapp. She drags them out of their shyness by encouraging them to wear play clothes made from drapes and leading them all in a series of songs. But there is trouble brewing, as the Nazis prepare to invade Austria. A very famous film, likely to meet with adult approval, though they and you will swiftly notice that it is almost *three hours long*. Suitable for all the family, though few of you will go the distance. The DVD includes a commentary track, documentary (it is based on a *true* story, after all), and interviews.

  Star rating: ✪✪✪

Space Camp
PG
Anchor Bay   1986
DVD; VHS

A group of American kids are chosen for the NASA space camp, where they are supposed to learn about the space program. Instead, they are accidentally launched into space and need to be talked out of orbit and out of danger. If you can cope with the 1980s fashions, this is good fun.

Star rating: ✪✪✪

Spy Kids
PG
Miramax Films   2001
DVD; VHS

Carmen and Juni Cortez find out that their parents are retired spies, who have been recalled to duty to prevent terrorists taking over the world with robot impostors of politicians. The children skip school, steal a rocket plane from their long-lost uncle Machete, and head off to help their parents. By turns funny and action-packed, a great one for all the spies in your family. Warm the cockles of your parents' hearts by saying "I always thought you looked like James Bond, Daddy." Watch for the scene where the kids have to get past "sleeping sharks" — real sharks need to keep moving or they suffocate!

 Star rating: ✪✪✪

Stand by Me
R
Columbia Pictures Industries   1986
DVD; VHS

A group of 12-year-old boys suspect that another kid has died in the woods and head off to look for him. Not suitable for younger kids, but those entering their teens will love it. The dead person, Ray Brauer, is named after a childhood friend of writer Stephen King, Raymond von Brauer, who was killed in a motorcycle accident. The Special Edition DVD includes a director's commentary, music video, and "Making of" documentary.

Star rating: ✪✪✪✪

Star Kid
PG
Trimark Pictures   1996
DVD; VHS

Young Spencer discovers an alien battle suit, sent to Earth by its creators, the Trelkins, to keep it from falling into the hands of the invading Brood. When a Brood warrior comes to Earth to claim it, Spencer dons the battle suit and fights him off, gaining the respect of his schoolmates. A modern update of

142

Flight of the Navigator, with more fighting in the style of the **Mighty Morphin Power Rangers**. There's nothing modern about the DVD extras though — you might as well just save money and get the VHS.

Star rating: ✪✪✪

Star Wars: Episode I — The Phantom Menace
PG
Twentieth Century Fox Film Corp.   **1999**
DVD; VHS

Jedi knights Qui-Gon and Obi-Wan must keep Queen Amidala safe from forces led by the evil Darth Maul and protect planet Naboo from attack. One of the few movies to benefit from being watched at home — it's a lot more fun when you can talk, wander out for food, pause, and ⏩ through any talky moments. Jump five minutes ahead every time you hear the word "midichlorian" — you won't miss much. Followed by *Star Wars: Episode II — Attack of the Clones*.

 Star rating: ✪✪✪✪

Star Wars: Episode IV — A New Hope
PG
Twentieth Century Fox Film Corp.   **1977**
DVD; VHS

Farmboy Luke Skywalker must rescue Princess Leia from Darth Vader's artificial moon, the Death Star. ⏩ to the escape from the Death Star, ready for the superb X-Wing fighter assault. The modern version of this film contains extra special-effects footage to keep it from looking dated next to its sequels. Watch for a moment when a soldier bangs his head on a doorframe — obviously he really *is* a little tall for a storm trooper.

 Star rating: ✪✪✪✪✪

Star Wars: Episode V — The Empire Strikes Back

PG
Twentieth Century Fox Film Corp.   1980
DVD; VHS

The Empire finally tracks down the Rebel Alliance to their latest hideout and, as the forces scatter, Luke Skywalker begins his Jedi training. Unexpected kissing stuff between "scoundrel" Han Solo and Princess Leia and a darker tone make this more popular with adults than with kids. But ❿ through Luke's night in the cold on the ice planet Hoth, ready for the fantastic Walker assault and the unforgettable chase through the asteroid field. Watch for the moment Han Solo is thrown into a prison cell at Cloud City — he almost pulls off one of the storm troopers' helmets, but they continue as if nothing has happened. Annoy adults by asking how long Luke's Jedi training takes — he can't have been doing it for more than a day before he's called away to rescue his friends.

 Star rating: ✪✪✪✪

The parents in MATILDA are played by Danny DeVito (who also directed the film) and his real-life wife Rhea Perlman (Carla from *Cheers*). They made the film because it was their daughter's favorite book.

Star Wars: Episode VI — Return of the Jedi
PG
Twentieth Century Fox Film Corp.   1983
DVD; VHS

Luke and his friends must rescue Han Solo from Jabba the Hutt, his former boss. Then the Rebel Alliance begins an assault on the Empire's new Death Star, with the Emperor himself on board. ◗◗ to the spectacular fight on Jabba the Hutt's Sail Barge and the climactic triple battle on, around, and on the world below the Death Star. The Ewoks also turn up in the **Ewok Adventure** movies.

 Star rating: ✪✪✪✪

Stuart Little
PG
Columbia Pictures   1999
DVD; VHS

George Little's parents adopt a mouse — Stuart — who's to be George's new brother. But Snowbell the cat, the family pet, soon becomes Stuart's deadly enemy. He plots to have Stuart kidnapped, killed, or otherwise removed, while George comes

145

to realize that he loves his new "brother" after all. Annoy adults by asking how Snowbell can put his collar back on again after he's lost it in the water. Followed by *Stuart Little 2*.

 Star rating: ✪✪✪

THEME NIGHT

Slight Night:
THE BORROWERS
HONEY, I SHRUNK THE KIDS
THUMBELINA
THE INDIAN IN THE
    CUPBOARD
STUART LITTLE

Suburban Commando
PG
New Line   1991
VHS

An interstellar warrior hides out on Earth with a normal family, until alien bounty hunters come to claim him. Since the alien warrior is played by former superstar wrestler Hulk Hogan, this involves a lot of fighting. Not very good, but the least-worst of Hogan's career, if that makes sense.

Star rating: ✪

The Swan Princess
New Line Cinema   1994
VHS

The evil sorcerer Rothbart transforms Princess Odette into a swan. She stays by the lake with her newfound animal friends Jean-Bob the frog, Speed the Turtle, and Puffin the bird. But then she meets Prince Derek, who promises to free her from the spell. A rather good retelling of the story of *Swan Lake*, complete with extra gags. That's the only "extra" you get though — the DVD version has nothing else but a trailer.

 Star rating: ✪✪✪

Swan Princess Escape from Castle Mountain
Warner Bros.   1997
VHS

Princess Odette must become a swan again in order to save Prince Derek's mother when she is kidnapped by evil sorcerer Clavius. A very bad case of sequelitis, and nowhere near as good as the first film. There is yet another sequel, imaginatively called *The Swan Princess III*, featuring yet another evil magician, Zelda the sorceress, kidnapping Odette (again!). There was also a *Swan Princess* sing-along video, which at least did the job of ▶**ing** for you to get to the songs.

 Star rating: ✪

Swiss Family Robinson
Walt Disney Productions/Buena   1960
VHS

Mother, father, and the three sons Robinson flee the danger of Napoleon for the safety of the South Seas. After being chased by pirates, they land at a beautiful paradise isle, where they proceed to settle down . . . though their adventures are by no means over. Still a winner, even so many years after it was made.

 Star rating: ✪✪✪

The Sword in the Stone
Walt Disney Productions/Buena   1963
DVD; VHS

Before he became king, Arthur was a lowly squire by the name of Wart, who is tutored by Merlin the wizard. His first adventure comes when Merlin's enemy Madame Mim challenges him to a magical duel. ◗ through the long early scenes in which Merlin wonders who will be coming to see him . . . what a waste of time. We want magic and mayhem, which does turn up . . . eventually. Some good extras on the DVD, including two bonus cartoons, a documentary about the Sherman brothers (who also wrote the music for **CHITTY CHITTY BANG BANG**), and a black-and-white guide to magic in Disney.

Star rating: ✪✪✪

Escape from the KIDS section #4: Musicals
Find yourself drawn to the song-and-dance numbers? Then get yourself *That's Entertainment!*, a two-part compilation of the best parts from many old musicals.

Tarzan

Buena Vista Pictures Distribution, Inc.   1999
DVD; VHS

Kala the gorilla loses her baby and adopts a human child whom she finds in a wrecked tree house. "Tarzan" grows up as a "white ape," until he realizes his true origins when a group of human hunters arrives in the jungle. Darker and grizzlier than the average Disney cartoon, and the songs are less related to events on-screen than in, say, **JUNGLE BOOK**. Look out for the scene where the humans' camp is wrecked and the tea set from **BEAUTY AND THE BEAST** puts in an appearance. The DVD is loaded with extras, including a "Making of," trivia game, read-along, and music video.

 Star rating: ✪✪✪

 Films do not always enjoy the same success worldwide — in France STAR WARS: EPISODE I — THE PHANTOM MENACE was beaten at the box office by ASTERIX AND OBELIX TAKE ON CAESAR.

Teenage Mutant Ninja Turtles

PG
New Line Cinema   1990
DVD; VHS

Mutant turtles Leonardo, Michelangelo, Raphael, and Donatello take on the Foot, a gang of evil ninja who are corrupting the children of New York. Plenty of fighting and gags in a film based on the 1980s comic. Definitely one for the family's kung-fu fanatics. And if you ever wondered what the turtles looked like out of their shells, the same actors also appear in the movie as the pizza delivery guy (Michelangelo), one of the youths harassing Splinter (Leonardo), and the guy in the taxi who yells at Raphael (Raphael!). The DVD includes a maze game and cast bios.

Star rating: ✪✪✪

Teenage Mutant Ninja Turtles II — The Secret of the Ooze
PG
New Line Cinema   1991
VHS

Shredder uses the same Ooze that mutated the turtles to turn himself into an even more powerful adversary . . . and then the fights start. Sadly, this film loses its way, dumping some of the action in favor of lame gags. Shame your parents by saying: "I like this rapper Vanilla Ice. Do you have any of his albums?" The fact that this is only around on bad old VHS ought to be a hint — not as good as the original, and a bad case of sequelitis.

Star rating: ✪

Teenage Mutant Ninja Turtles III
PG
New Line Cinema   1993
VHS

For this second sequel, the turtles are whisked away from their New York home to medieval Japan, into the middle of a feud between rival warlords. Which means even more fighting

(Cowabunga!), but also an increased kiddification of the humor. Fans of the first movie will be pleased to see self-proclaimed superhero Casey Jones return, but he's not around for the whole film. A terminal case of sequelitis that killed the franchise, though the long-running cartoon series is around for those who can't get enough of it. Rumors abound, however, that the creators are seeking to bring the turtles back from the dead in computer-animated form.

Star rating: ✪

Thomas and the Magic Railroad
Destination Film Distribution Company, Inc.   **2000**
DVD; VHS

Thomas the Tank Engine lives in the world of Sodor, a magical place where locomotives talk. Mr. Conductor can travel between Sodor and our world with his magic gold dust, but his supply is running out. He goes in search of a new way to pass between the worlds, but the rogue train Diesel is also looking for it. An unnecessarily complicated attempt to integrate *Thomas the Tank Engine* with real-life people — but wasn't *Thomas* supposed to take place in our world anyway? What's all this Sodor nonsense?

Star rating: ✪

The Three Caballeros
Walt Disney Productions/Buena   **1944**
DVD; VHS

Donald Duck opens his presents on his birthday and watches some films on his new movie projector before being whisked away to Mexico, where he falls in love. An explosive combination of song-and-dance numbers that whips past your eyes before you can take it all in. You'll be needing the *rewind* button to appreciate all the good points of this one.

Star rating: ✪✪✪

Thumbelina
Warner Bros.   1993
DVD; VHS

A woman wishes for a daughter, but when she gets one, she's only six inches tall. Though Thumbelina meets a handsome prince, she is kidnapped by toads and harrassed by a vole. Only her prince can save her, but he has been trapped in a block of ice. A romantic cartoon from the people who brought you **ALL DOGS GO TO HEAVEN**.

 Star rating: ✪✪

Thunderbirds Are Go
Carlton/AP Films/Century 21   1966
VHS

The International Rescue team is called in to supervise the launch of the Zero-X rocket after the prototype meets with a suspicious accident. One of two feature follow-ups to the *Thunderbirds* TV show (the other is *Thunderbird 6*), this puppet movie is sadly showing its age when compared to the special effects of animation, computer graphics, and muppetry. Certain adults will be eager to see it because they remember loving *Thunderbirds* as kids, but you may find other things to keep you entertained . . . this does go on a bit. Get it as a treat for your parents, not for you.

Star rating: ✪✪

A Tiger Walks
PRD   1964
VHS

A tiger escapes from a circus truck and hides out in the woods. You'd think that was a recipe for a horror movie, but instead the local children decide the tiger must have been cruelly treated and try to buy it from its former owners. A little old-fashioned, but nice for the animal lovers.

Star rating: ✪✪

The Tigger Movie
Buena Vista Pictures Distribution, Inc.   2000
DVD; VHS

Tigger (a friend of Winnie the Pooh) misses his family and mistakenly believes that they are coming to visit. His friends dress up as tiggers, but he sees through their disguises and sets off to see if he can find a real family of tiggers he can bounce with. The DVD extras include a sing-along section, storybook, music video, and games. Fun, especially for the younger tiggers in your own family.

   Star rating: ✪✪✪

Time Bandits

PG

Avco Embassy Pictures   1981

DVD; VHS

Average schoolboy Kevin falls in with six dwarfs who are fleeing from the Supreme Being. Their only guide — a map to all the time holes in the universe, which takes them from ancient Greece to medieval Sherwood Forest, with stopovers on the *Titanic*, a meeting with Napoleon at the Battle of Castiglione, and all points in between. A fabulously grim comedy from the Monty Python people — scary for the young ones but timeless fun for older bandits. The Criterion DVD contains a detailed commentary for the grown-ups, but little else except a "scrapbook" of photos for the kids.

 Star rating: ✪✪✪✪

 STAR WARS: EPISODE IV — A NEW HOPE was inspired by a Japanese samurai film, *Hidden Fortress*, about two bunglers and a tough guy who rescue a beautiful princess from a secret prison.

Titan A.E.

PG

Twentieth Century Fox Film Corp.   2000

DVD; VHS

Fifteen years after Earth is destroyed by the evil Drej, human survivor Cale discovers that his father's ring could hold the key to uniting humanity — but only if he reaches the Titan vessel that can create a new planet. Sci-fi hokum loaded with computer graphics — one for older viewers. Watch for the moment when Stith claims they are out of ammo — the gun indicators seem to disagree with her in the next shot! The special edition DVD includes a commentary, a "Making of," a music video, and a picture gallery — strangely disappointing.

 Star rating: ✪✪✪

Tom and Jerry: The Movie
Turner Entertainment Co.   1992
VHS

Thrown out on the streets, old enemies Tom and Jerry must work together to survive. Befriending human runaway Robyn, they are captured by her evil aunt. Escaping from an animal prison, they end up back at Robyn's house, where they can be enemies once more, just like old times. A strangely lame outing for the famous cat-and-mouse duo, silent for decades and suddenly given voices so they can talk to each other in this movie edition. And anyway, you watch T&J because you want to see them hit each other with frying pans and anvils, not "cooperate" like refugees from *Sesame Street*. Right? Fourteen of T&J's earlier adventures are compiled on another DVD, *Tom & Jerry's Greatest Chases*, which is much more fun.

Star rating: ✪✪

Toy Story
Buena Vista Pictures Distribution, Inc.   1995
DVD; VHS

Andy's favorite toy, Woody the Cowboy, is supplanted in his owner's affections by Buzz

Lightyear, a space-warrior action figure who believes he's a *real* space ranger — not a toy! But all the toys band together when Andy moves, and they risk being left behind with Sid the toy butcher. A wonderful feature for all the family, and the first to exclusively use computer animation. Look for the massive pile-up Scud and Buzz cause at the intersection — you can hear it, but the cars don't actually crash! The DVD includes the *Tin Toy* short that inspired the movie, commentaries, a "Making of," and even an interview with Buzz and Woody. Buzz Lightyear returns in his own series, *Buzz Lightyear of Star Command*, but it's nowhere near as good as the original movie.

 Star rating: ✪✪✪✪✪

Toy Story 2
Buena Vista Pictures Distribution Inc.   1999
DVD; VHS

Left behind when Andy goes to camp, Woody is discovered by a greedy toy shop owner and collector who realizes he is a valuable "collector's item" and plans to sell him to a Japanese toy museum. A rare case of a sequel with all the excitement of the original — by turns fun and weepily sentimental. You will never see your toys in the same way again. Budding doctor types can ask themselves: "If Woody tears his arm at the beginning and can't use it, how come he *can* when it gets torn again by Stinky Pete near the end?" The DVD features the short film *Luxo Jr.* that was the company's first ever production, fake outtakes, and a trailer for **Monsters Inc**. *Toy Story 2* is available with the first film in a special "Ultimate Toy Box" edition, which includes an entire disc of additional stuff — an absolutely massive treasure trove of extras, ensuring this is one toy you won't be leaving forgotten under the bed.

 Star rating: ✪✪✪✪✪

The Transformers — The Movie
PG
DeLaurentiis Entertainment Group   1986
DVD; VHS

The Autobots and Decepticons, battling groups of transforming robots, continue their ongoing war on their home world of Cybertron. But this time, the Decepticons are the unwitting dupes of Unicron, an evil being that needs to remove the Autobots who can stop it. Showing its age, but still packing a punch for fans of robot fighting, this cartoon also features some famous voices, including the gravelly Orson Welles and Leonard "Spock" Nimoy. Watch for the robots being dipped into acid soon after Daniel has been swept away — do my eyes deceive me, or is that . . . Daniel watching them? DVD extras include storyboards and an interview with the composer. The *Transformers* TV series has gone through many incarnations and continues today — other releases include *Beast Wars*, *Headmasters,* and *Robots in Disguise*.

Star rating: ✪✪✪

Tron
PG
Walt Disney Productions/Buena   1982
VHS

Flynn the computer hacker is thrown into a digital world where the evil Master Control Program is

trying to seize control. Accompanied by Tron, a
program he created, he fights his way across the
glowing landscape, hoping to escape and maybe
save the planet. ⏵ to the light-cycle contest — a
superb racing sequence. Tron still has an amazing
look — shot with real people but then colored to
look like a computer-generated film. Sadly, the
sleight-of-hand continues in the DVD release —
packaged to look like a 21st-century DVD, but with
no extras you wouldn't find on a 1980s VHS. Look
out for the image of Mickey Mouse picked out in
lights far below the characters' ship — yes, this is
a Disney film. A sequel, *Tron 2.0*, is currently in
production.

Star rating: ✪✪✪

Byte Night:

TRON

TOY STORY

A BUG'S LIFE

SMALL SOLDIERS

FINAL FANTASY: THE SPIRITS WITHIN

THEME
NIGHT

Twenty Thousand Leagues Under the Sea

Walt Disney Productions/Buena   1954
VHS

In 1868, the people of San Francisco live in fear of a sea monster preying on local ships. The "sea monster" (really a submarine called the *Nautilus*) destroys the warship sent to kill it, and only a handful of people survive. They are taken on board by Captain Nemo, a maverick intent on stopping warfare at sea. Watch out for an impressive fight with a giant squid. Confound adults by saying: "Wasn't Captain Nemo supposed to be Asian?" He was in the original books.

 Star rating: ✪✪✪

Wallace and Gromit

Aardman   1992
DVD; VHS

Lovable inventor Wallace and his no-nonsense dog Gromit are no strangers to adventures — heading for the moon in *A Grand Day Out*, fighting a penguin criminal in *The Wrong Trousers*, and protecting a hapless sheep (called Sean) in *A Close Shave*. Superb plasticine animation from the people who brought you **CHICKEN RUN**. Though available separately on VHS, the best way to enjoy W&G is on the DVD compilation, which throws all three of their first adventures onto a single disc. It also includes test footage, a "Making of," and, for the British version, the BBC Christmas graphics that used W&G one year.

 Star rating: ✪✪✪✪✪

WarGames

PG

MGM/UA Entertainment Co.   1983

DVD; VHS

"Shall — we — play — a — game?" Schoolboy
David Lightman finds a secret way into a
government supercomputer and asks it if it wants
to play. The computer decides to play "World War
Three," and David must stop it before trouble
breaks out for real. One of the earliest and best
movies about computer hacking — the hardware
might look antique now, but the story is still
excellent, particularly for older viewers. The militarily
minded may like to wonder why the General
orders "Send out the F-16s," but we see F-15s
taking off. A court-martial for air traffic control,
there. The DVD includes a commentary, but not
much else.

 Star rating: ✪✪✪✪

Warriors of Virtue

PG

MGM/UA Distribution Co.   1997

VHS

Earth boy Ryan falls into a whirlpool and wakes up
in the magical Land of Tao. He joins the four
Warriors of Virtue, kangaroo kung-fu masters, on a
quest to defeat the evil Komodo before he can
take over the world. Martial arts action from Hong
Kong, for everyone who still likes the **MIGHTY
MORPHIN POWER RANGERS**. Good fights, stinky story.

Star rating: ✪✪✪

The Watcher in the Woods
PG
Walt Disney Productions/Buena   1980
VHS

An American family moves into an old English
house, where one daughter sees visions of a girl
who disappeared many years before, while
another *hears* her. A creepy film likely to give
younger viewers the heebie-jeebies (and quite a
few older ones, too). Preserve super-creepy status
by **-ing** every time the dog turns up or the
parents start wasting time. You want to see the
children and their quest to unravel the mystery
before it's too late! Even the *music* is scary.

Star rating: ✪✪✪

The Water Babies
MGM/Ariadne/Studio Minotaur   1978
DVD; VHS

Accused of a crime he didn't commit, Tom the
chimney sweep throws himself into a river. He
cannot return to the surface until he finds the
"water babies," so he begins looking for them
underwater, accompanied by a lobster and a sea
horse. A strange mix of live-action above the
waterline and animated cartoon below, with some

THEME NIGHT

Bleak Week:
BAMBI
WATERSHIP DOWN
WHISTLE DOWN THE WIND
OLD YELLER

old-fashioned attitudes that really make this film look even older than it really is.

 Star rating: ✪

Watership Down

PG

Avco Embassy Pictures   1978

VHS

The rabbits' warren is under threat from builders, so Hazel leads them to safety, risking danger from rats, cats, and even human beings. But the deadliest threat comes from Woundwort, the tyrant of the local rabbits, who must be defeated before the creatures of Hazel's burrow can be truly safe. Though the adventures of cartoon bunnies might sound fluffy beyond belief, *Watership Down* is a serious film and can often be dark and scary. At the time this film was released, people complained that it was too scary for kids and too childish for adults. Not much has changed, though there is now also a cutesified TV series.

 Star rating: ✪✪✪

When the Whales Came

PG

Twentieth Century Fox Film Corp.   1989

VHS

During the First World War, a pair of children in the Scilly Isles befriend Birdman, an old man who lives on the coast. When narwhals are washed up on the beach, the local community of scavengers prepares to kill them for food, but Birdman warns that killing the whales will have dire consequences — ones that already destroyed the livelihood of a neighboring isle 70 years earlier. A little slow-moving, but suspenseful.

Star rating: ✪✪

Whistle Down the Wind
Winstone/Cinema Club   1961
VHS

Kathy finds a man hiding in her family's barn and becomes convinced that he is Jesus. She hopes that he will cure her sick kittens, though the local police have other ideas about the man's identity. Deep and touching stuff — well worth enduring in black and white. Based on the book by Mary Hayley Bell (mother of Hayley Mills, who plays Kathy), which has a slightly different ending. There is also a 1994 remake, not currently available on video, and an Andrew Lloyd Webber musical version.

Star rating: ✪✪✪✪

Who Framed Roger Rabbit?
PG
Buena Vista Pictures Distribution, Inc.   1988
DVD; VHS

Roger Rabbit, a down-on-his-luck cartoon character from Toon Town, hires real-life human detective Eddie Valiant to save him from a murder charge. But Eddie has a grudge against "toons" (one killed his brother) and is reluctant to help. A superb return to the style and comedy of old-time cartoons like *Bugs Bunny*, mixed with real actors and more than a few walk-ons from cartoon stars of yesteryear — watch out for Dumbo, Betty Boop, and Droopy. Astound your parents by noting that Sylvester, Yosemite Sam, and Road Runner had not been created in 1944, when the film they appear in is supposedly set. The animation was supervised by Richard Williams, who also made **ARABIAN KNIGHT**. No extras on the DVD, though — a very poor showing.

 Star rating: ✪✪✪✪

 E.T. THE EXTRA TERRESTRIAL had several title changes before director Steven Spielberg settled on the final one. They included *Night Skies*, *A Boy's Life*, and *E.T. and Me*.

Wide Awake
PG
Miramax Films   1996
DVD; VHS

Ten-year-old Joshua goes looking for the meaning of life after his grandfather dies, causing havoc at his Catholic school as he tries different religions, falls in love, and learns how to steer a bucket on wheels. A touching and funny film about growing up. Amaze adults by revealing this was the debut of M. Night Shyamalan, who would later make a very different film about a boy who talks to dead people — *The Sixth Sense*. Someone who definitely wasn't wide awake was working on the DVD — there are no worthwhile extras.

 Star rating: ✪✪✪✪

Willow

PG
MGM Pictures   1988
VHS

A fantasy version of **Star Wars**, loaded with swordfights, magic, and chases. Wicked queen Bavmorda orders the death of all the local children, but one child is rescued by Willow the Nelwyn. He decides to return her to her people, accompanied by a shape-shifting sorceress, a good-for-nothing swordsman, and Bavmorda's own rebellious daughter. ⏩ to the incredible battle at the castle, which is attacked by a two-headed dragon.

 Star rating: ✪✪✪✪

Willy Wonka and the Chocolate Factory

Paramount Pictures Corp.   1971
DVD; VHS

Young Charlie joins four other children who find the Golden Tickets and win a once-in-a-lifetime trip to

Willie Wonka's famous chocolate factory. But the factory is not just a paradise of cakes and candy. It can be a terrifying place where bad little children get exactly what they deserve! Dark and disturbing fun, and not for the fainthearted. You can see the joins though — watch when Violet starts chewing the blueberry gum, and you will see the special-effects tube going up her leg to make her expand. Whoever decided the DVD shouldn't have any extras deserves a one-way trip to the chocolate factory.

   Star rating: ✪✪✪

THEME NIGHT

Spite Night (Roald Dahl films):
MATILDA
WITCHES
JAMES AND THE GIANT PEACH
CHITTY CHITTY BANG BANG (HE
   WROTE THE SCRIPT, YOU KNOW)
WILLIE WONKA AND THE CHOCOLATE
   FACTORY

The Wind in the Willows
PG
Columbia Pictures   1996
VHS

Toad sells land to the weasels, who disturb Mole's spring cleaning with their bulldozers. But Toad doesn't care, because his new interest is motoring. Then it becomes clear that the weasels want to demolish Toad Hall and replace it with a dog food factory. A live-action adaptation of Kenneth

Grahame's famous children's books, with some famous English names in the cast.

Star rating: ✪✪✪

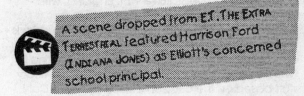

A scene dropped from E.T. THE EXTRA TERRESTRIAL featured Harrison Ford (INDIANA JONES) as Elliott's concerned school principal.

Winnie the Pooh
Walt Disney Productions/Buena   1968–1988
VHS

After a failed attempt to steal honey from a beehive, Winnie the Pooh rolls in mud, grabs a balloon, and unconvincingly poses as a cloud. That's *Winnie the Pooh and the Honey Tree*, only one of several Disney adaptations of the famous A. A. Milne stories about Christopher Robin's bear. There's also *Winnie the Pooh and the Blustery Day*, in which the forest is flooded, *Winnie the Pooh and Tigger Too*, in which Pooh and Piglet try to find a way to stop Tigger bouncing, and *The Many Adventures of Winnie the Pooh*, which collects some of the short cartoon adventures. There are also many videos, and the much later TIGGER MOVIE. A treat for all fans of the bear with little brain, his miserable friend Eeyore, wise Owl, and the other occupants of the Hundred Acre Wood. Currently unavailable on DVD, but surely it's only a matter of time.

 Star rating: ✪✪✪

The Witches

PG

Warners Bros.   1989

DVD; VHS

Orphan Luke moves to Brighton, England, with
his sick grandmother. At the same time, a
national witch conference on capturing children is
underway. When Luke discovers the witches hiding
at his hotel, they turn him into a mouse, making it
twice as difficult to thwart their evil scheme. Scary
stuff based on the children's book by Roald Dahl.
The author said he didn't think this film was funny
enough, but most of the audience seemed to like
it anyway. But if you read the book first, you may
surprised by how "nice" the new ending is.

 Star rating: ✪✪✪

The Wizard of Oz

MGM Film Company   1939

DVD; VHS

Kansas schoolgirl Dorothy Gale is snatched away in
a tornado and transported to the magical land of
Oz. To get home, she needs to follow the Yellow
Brick Road to the Emerald City and ask the all-
powerful Wizard for his help. But as she sets off,
accompanied by her friends Scarecrow, Tin Man,
and the Cowardly Lion, she is pursued by the
Wicked Witch, who wants her ruby slippers. It starts
in black and white before exploding into riotous
color, so you can imagine what effect this had on
audiences back in drab 1939. It's still a winner,
even though it's older than your grandparents.
"Over the Rainbow" won an Oscar for best song.
There have also been several cartoon series, a
streetwise musical version (*The Wiz*), and a

Japanese sci-fi remake — *Galaxy Adventures of Space Oz*. The DVD is great, with a documentary, deleted scenes, outtakes, clips from other versions, and even clips from the 1939 Oscars.

  Star rating: ✪✪✪✪✪

The CAT FROM OUTER SPACE was actually played by a brother and sister — Rumpler and Amber.

Wombling Free
Winstone   1977
VHS

The Wombles (Great Uncle Bulgaria, Orinoco, Tobermory, Madame Cholet, et al.) are creatures that clean up the trash on Wimbledon Common, but no human can see them . . . or so they think. Young Kim Frogmorton invites Bungo to tea, and her parents eventually admit that they can see him, too. The Frogmorton family decides to help

★★★★★★★★★★★★★★★★★★★★★★★★★★★★★★
★ **Credit watching:** A "Producer" can be
★ anything, including the person who had
★ the original idea, the one who actually
★ paid for the film to be made, or even just
★ the director's girlfriend. It's what they call
★ someone when they can't think of what
★ else to call them. It's best not to mess
★ with them, though.
★★★★★★★★★★★★★★★★★★★★★★★★★★★★★★

the Wombles in their clean-up operation, but will other human beings be able to see them? You may not be able to see them unless you find them on TV — this video isn't available yet in the United States. But that may be no big loss — this film does seem to go on a little too long.

Star rating: ✪✪

Young Sherlock Holmes
PG-13
Paramount Pictures Corp.   1985
VHS

Sherlock Holmes and John Watson, two boys at a British boarding school, investigate strange goings-on as a sinister cabal of businessmen becomes involved in an Egyptian death cult. Good fun from the people who brought you **GOONIES**, with plenty of in-jokes as the teenage Holmes assembles many of the clothes and items that become his trademark in adulthood.

Star rating: ✪✪✪

Sources

Handy reference materials for writing this book included the *Time Out Film Guide* (Penguin), *The Virgin Film Guide* (Virgin), *Now Showing 2: A Directory of Films for Children* (BFI), and the *Ultimate DVD Guide* (Titan). Further advice for adults can be found in *The Parent's Guide to the Best Family Movies* (Griffin) and *The Movie Mom's Video Guide to Family Movies* (Avon).

For information, viewer opinions, and ordering information on-line, **www.amazon.com** (United States), **www.amazon.co.uk** (United Kingdom), and **www.dvdpacific.com** (Australia) are invaluable. Another good information source is the International Movie Database at **www.imdb.com,** while information on the best and worst of DVDs can be found at **www.digitallyobsessed.com** and **www.dvdreview.com**. On-line advice for parents is at **www.gradingthemovies.com** and **www.cqcm.org**. Gossip on hidden extras and in-jokes can be found on-line at **www.eeggs.com**, while you can catch out people's mistakes at **www.slipups.com**. If you're still lost and want to search the Web for other opinions, then the best place to start is **www.google.com**.

Ten of the best...

My Neighbor Totoro
A Bug's Life
Stand by Me
Shrek
Star Wars: Episode IV — A New Hope
Toy Story (1 and 2)
Wallace and Gromit
Babe
The Iron Giant
Lord of the Rings: The Fellowship of
  the Ring

Ten of the worst...

BMX Bandits
Digimon: The Movie
Freddie as F.R.O.7
GoBots: Battle of the Rock Lords
Mac and Me
Pokémon, The First Movie
My Little Pony — The Movie
Thomas and the Magic Railroad
Surburban Commando
The Water Babies

TOP TENS

Ten Oldies...

Chitty Chitty Bang Bang
Doctor Dolittle (1967)
Jason and the Argonauts
Lassie Come Home
National Velvet
The Railway Children
Snow White and the Seven
   Dwarfs
The Sound of Music
The Wizard of Oz
Whistle Down the Wind

Ten fantasy faves...

The Lord of the Rings:
   Fellowship of the Ring
Dragonheart
Willow
The Lion, the Witch, and
   the Wardrobe
Dragonslayer
Labyrinth
Ladyhawke
Quest for Camelot
Arabian Knight
Warriors of Virtue

TOP TENS

Ten scary movies...

The Watcher in the Woods
Men In Black
Matilda
The Nightmare Before Christmas
Watership Down
The Addams Family
Addams Family Values
Indiana Jones and the Raiders of
    the Lost Ark
Indiana Jones and the Temple of
    Doom
Lord of the Rings: The Fellowship
    of the Ring

Ten science fiction faves...

E.T. The Extraterrestrial
Star Wars I: The Phantom Menace
Star Wars IV: A New Hope
Star Wars V: The Empire Strikes Back
Star Wars VI: Return of the Jedi
The Last Starfighter
The Transformers — The Movie
Tron
Wargames
Dexter's Laboratory: Ego Trip

TOP TENS

Ten sequels...

Toy Story 2
Back to the Future Part II
Back to the Future Part III
The Lost World: Jurassic Park
Lady and the Tramp II:
    Scamp's Adventure
The Little Mermaid 2
The Return of Jafar
Aladdin and the King of
    Thieves
Swan Princess Escape from
    Castle Mountain
Free Willy 2: The Adventure
    Home

Ten animal movies...

Babe
Cats & Dogs
101 Dalmatians
The Wind in the Willows
Lassie Come Home
Watership Down
National Velvet
Digby the Biggest Dog in the
    World
Black Beauty
Far From Home: The
    Adventure of Yellow Dog

TOP TENS

Ten musicals...

The Jungle Book
The Sound of Music
Mary Poppins
The King and I
Beauty and the Beast
Annie
The Lion King
Doctor Dolittle (1967)
The Muppet Movie
Shrek

TOP TENS